The
Job Support Machine

A Critique of the Subsidy Morass

JOHN BURTON

Centre for Policy Studies
London 1979

First published 1979
by Centre for Policy Studies
Wilfred Street, London SW1

© Centre for Policy Studies

ISBN 0 905880 15 3 (hardback)
    0 905880 14 5 (softback)

Typeset and printed by
Orchard & Ind Ltd., Gloucester

Publication by the Centre for Policy Studies does not imply
acceptance of authors' conclusions or prescriptions. They are
chosen for their ability to make an independent and
intellectually rigorous contribution to debate on economic
social and political issues.

Contents

FOREWORD by Sir Arnold Weinstock   v

I.   **THE ENCROACHING MORASS**   1

     The Subsidy Morass in British Industry
     How Much Does the Subsidy Morass Cost?
     The 'New' Industrial Strategy: More of the Same
     The International Context

II.   **RATIONALES FOR INDUSTRIAL SUBSIDIES: A**   11
    A CRITICAL APPRAISAL

     THE JOBS RATIONALE
         Job Subsidies and Employment
         Job Subsidies and Inflation
         Job Subsidies and the Budget Deficit
         Conclusion on Job Rationale

     THE NEW INDUSTRIAL POLICY RATIONALE
         The Evolution of NIP in the UK
         The Arguments for NIP
         The Arguments Examined
         Conclusion on NIP

     THE BALANCE OF PAYMENTS RATIONALE

     THE NATIONAL INTEREST RATIONALE

     GENERAL CONCLUSION ON THE RATIONALE OF
     INDUSTRIAL SUBSIDIES

III. **THE POLITICAL ECONOMY OF THE SUBSIDY MORASS**   41

Government Motivation, Political Bias and Encroaching
     Subsidization
Reinforcing Factors
Conclusion

IV. **THE CONSEQUENCES OF CONTINUED ENCROACHMENT**   47

The Long-Term Effects on Business Behaviour
The Long-Term Effects on Employee and Union Behaviour
The Long-Term Effects on the Process of Economic
     Evolution
The Long-Term Effects on Government-Industry Relations
The Long-Term Effects on the International Economy and
     Polity
Conclusion: The Dangers of Engulfment

V. **ON ESCAPING THE MORASS**   59

Some Positive Policy Proposals

Conclusion

FOOTNOTES   65

REFERENCES   67

Foreword

Foreword by Sir Arnold Weinstock

There has always been argument about how much the State should do for, or with, or to, industry. Between the theoretical extremes of the planned, state-controlled Leviathan economy on the one hand, and the atomistic, uncontrolled "free" economy on the other, there exists that wide grey area in which most of the world's economies actually exist. Governments, in the face of political realities, are obliged to some extent to participate in the industrial affairs of the country. But fundamental economic laws do not obey any government *fiat*, and all experience tells us that governments are not competent to manufacture goods or to develop new products and new markets. This is not to say that they cannot be helpful to industry, for example by maintaining a stable economic environment and by allowing adequate rewards to those who actually do the job.

Few in the private sector presently believe that government participation in industrial affairs since, say, 1950 has been soundly conceived or effectively implemented. The post-war period has been marked by the inability of governments to achieve, whether by direct or indirect means, the desired improvement in Britain's productiveness and competitiveness. Government intervention in industry is invariably incompetent, and this applies to government subsidy as to every other form of arbitrary interference with the economy.

John Burton's paper is welcome as one of the first attempts to give a comprehensive account of the accelerating trend towards subsidising the inefficient and the unproductive. It should help to contribute to a better understanding of some of the effects of the present "industrial strategy" as well as the misconceptions inherent in many of the arguments canvassed in its support.

I. The Encroaching Morass

Public discussion and academic analysis of government intervention in industry both tend, inevitably, to focus on its more overt forms, such as nationalization and price and wage controls. However, one of the most important growth areas of government involvement in industry today is less conspicuous: in Britain – and many other countries – industry is becoming increasingly permeated by a morass of government subsidies. The purpose of this study is to examine this important yet insufficiently-understood phenomenon, to consider its supposed rationale, and to analyse its consequences for the economy, for policy, and for society.

The Subsidy Morass in British Industry

The disbursement of a morass of subsidies to industry is a comparatively recent phenomenon in Britain. In the 1950s there were large government subsidies to the nationalized industries – often hidden in the form of low-cost loans and capital write-offs – but the private sector operated largely without any such system of government bounty. The cotton textile industry, facing contraction as a result of low-price import competition, was the exception to the general rule, receiving subsidies under the 1948 Cotton Spinning (Re-Equipment Subsidy) Act, and the 1959 Cotton Industry Act. But the overall picture in that decade, at least in the private sector, was one of modest and, indeed, comparatively trivial levels of government subsidization of industry.

Since the mid-1960s this picture has changed dramatically. Government subsidy schemes, to promote this, that, and the other, have multiplied and expanded at a dizzying and accelerating rate, reaching a crescendo of sorts within the last few years. It is now difficult not to open a newspaper or some official magazine such as the Department of Employment's *Gazette* without learning of some new programme of subsidies being dreamed up by the Manpower Services Commission or the Department of Trade and Industry, the decision to 'extend' an existent scheme in some manner, or the announcement of some new 'package' of subsidy measures by the Treasury.

Such has been the speed with which this subsidy morass has advanced that its true nature is not fully realized either by the general public or by the economics' profession. As one authority on public finance, Professor Carl Shoup of Columbia University, noted a few years ago: ' . . . subsidies are the great fiscal unknown . . . most public finance textbooks . . . do not even list the word "subsidy" in their indices, or give only a page or two of references. There has been no monograph on subsidies in the English language . . . it is really astonishing' (Shoup, (1972).[1] Although some economic research on the effect of industrial subsidies on international trade has appeared in recent years as a result of studies sponsored by the Trade Policy Research Centre in London, subsidies still remain largely as the 'great fiscal unknown' to the public, press, and economists alike.

Another factor that has hindered a fuller appreciation of the true extent of the subsidy morass is that many subsidies are hidden in the form of "soft" (i.e. below-market cost) government loans, "free" (i.e. tax-financed) government provision of industrial advice to businesses, "preferential" treatment of domestically-produced goods in government purchasing programmes, and so on. To capture the full picture it is therefore necessary to define an industrial subsidy as any government measure which reduces the costs of production of a firm or industry below that level which would have obtained in the absence of the measure.

Merely to describe all of the government measures adopted in Britain over, say, the past two decades which fall within this definition, let alone to describe the unending policy switches between one measure and another that have also taken place, would in itself require a monograph. Perhaps a simple list of the major industrial subsidy measures which have been applied to British industry during this time period will give an idea of the byzantine complexity of the encroaching subsidy morass:[2] initial and accelerated depreciation allowances (at varying rates) for investment, free depreciation on industrial plant in "development

2

districts", tax-free cash grants for investments; investment allowances; regional development grants; building grants; plant and machinery grants; removal and resettlement grants for "key" workers where a firm is moving to an "assisted area"; operating grants; interest relief grants; "favourable" (i.e. subsidized) government loans; "financial support" for certain industries – most particularly, shipbuilding, cotton textiles, aircraft, computers, and primary aluminium smelting; government purchase and free loan to user firms of machine tools and other manufacturing equipment; aircraft "launching" aid; *ad hoc* "rescue operations" by government involving staggering public subsidies in the cases of large firms like B L, Rolls Royce, Upper Clyde Shipbuilders, Ferranti and Alfred Herbert; "special" government "assistance" to the wool industry; grants and "soft" loans for "modernization" and "restructuring" of "important" sectors of industry such as ball-bearings production, instrument engineering, paper, textiles, and car assemblage; grants for the construction of small factories in rural areas; "assistance" in the stockpiling of machine tools; grants for the improvement of public sector housing – as an aid for the construction industry; grants to firms for training or retraining of employees; subsidies to industrial research and development work through government purchasing programmes and other means; mergers lubricated by taxpayers' money in the computer and other industries; loans and credit guarantees for the Concorde and the QEII; central government grants to local authorities to provide better facilities for industry in "development" areas; rent-free periods for firms renting government factories in special development areas; "special" grants for building on derelict land; grants for "rationalization" measures in industry where this would "safeguard employment"; development agency grants for the establishment of new industrial estates and purpose-built factories; government "support" for "industrial innovation" in the aero-space and nuclear power industries; "free" provision of industrial advice by government-financed bureaucracies such as the "industrial expansion teams", "development agencies", and "regional development grants offices"; service industry grants; regional employment "premiums"; "temporary" employment subsidies for firms retaining employees that were to be made redundant; subsidies for employing school-leavers and unemployed youths; subsidies to small firms taking on extra employees; vast subsidies in the form of capital write-offs, public dividend capital and soft loans in the nationalized industries – indeed the very nationalization of many industries and firms, such as B L and British Shipbuilding, has carried with it an explicit or implicit political commitment to subsequent subsidization; government "injections" of equity finance into private-sector companies via the 1972 Industry Act and the National Enterprise Board; subsidies for worker-control "experiments" in ailing firms such as Meriden, Kirkby Manufacturing, and the *Scottish Daily News*; implicit subsidies via government direction of the supposedly-autonomous nationalized industry boards to place orders with companies that have spare capacity (e.g. the Drax B power station order for Parsons; the BNOC drilling-rig order for Marathon Shipbuilding); subsidies for exports via the government-financed exports credit guarantee scheme; the "sale" of British ships to foreign commercial fleets at subsidized prices (e.g. the Polish ships 'deal'); subsidies to firms providing "work experience" for unemployed adolescents; building subsidies for the hotel industry; and *etcetera, etcetera, etcetera* . . .

On top of these subsidies programmes for industry, recent years have also seen the implementation of large subsidy programmes to promote employment in non-commercial activities, such as the job creation programme and the "community industry" scheme run by the Manpower Services Commission.

How Much Does the Subsidy Morass Cost?

It is in itself a significant commentary on the situation that neither the British Government nor anyone else knows with any precision how much it is spending on the morass of subsidy schemes listed above. Some idea can be gleaned from the figures for government expenditure on "trade, industry and employment" published each year in the annual Public Expenditure Survey Committee (PESC) White Paper. The figures for such expenditures for the period 1970-71 to 1975-76, contained in the 1976 PESC White Paper are reprinted here as Table I.[3]

As this table shows, government expenditure on promoting 'trade, industry, and employment' has grown very rapidly over recent years. Indeed it has been one of the fastest-growing elements in total public expenditure over the past decade and more. During the period 1969-

70 to 1974-75 it grew 63 per cent at constant (1974) prices, and during the period 1970-71 to 1975-76 it grew 44 per cent at constant (1975) prices.[4]

The figures in Table I, however, both understate and overstate the size of the subsidy morass in British industry. They overstate the size of government subsidies to industry in that not all loan assistance to industry is pure subsidy; some government loans contain large elements of subsidy (i.e. the interest rate set by government is way below the level that obtains on comparable loans raised in the capital market), others little or none. But the figures also understate the size of government subsidy measures in that they do not include implicit government subsidies in the form of tax relief for industry and subsidies hidden in "preferential" purchasing policies adopted by government or forced by it on the nationalized industries. These latter hidden subsidies could be quite large as the central government alone purchases over one-tenth of all manufacturing output in Britain, while the six largest nationalized industries alone account for approximately one-third of expenditure on plant and equipment in the United Kingdom.

Making proper allowances for these factors in order to gauge the true extent of the subsidy morass in British industry is decidedly difficult. In the case of many government loans to industry the terms of the loan are deliberately concealed in order to hide the subsidy element. And even where the terms of such loans have been made known publicly this does not mean that they are actually stuck to! Many a government loan to public and private industry is subsequently "softened" by commutation, postponement of repayments, or by subsequent substitution of loan finance by government equity finance. Again, it is almost impossible to discover the volume of subsidies hidden in preferential purchasing policies adopted in the public sector. However, an heroic effort has been made by Denton, O'Cleireacain and Ash (1975) to take some of these factors into account. Their study attempts to estimate the subsidy element in government loans to industry, and to add in implicit subsidies in the form of indirect tax relief, to get a better picture of the size of government subsidies to industry. On this basis they estimate that industrial subsidy measures amounted to approximately 7 per cent of the central government's budget in the United Kingdom during 1970-71

Table 1

Government Expenditure on Trade, Industry and Employment

	1970-71	1971-72	1972-73	1973-74	1974-75	1975-76
Regional support and regeneration						
Regional development grants	—	—	10.8	109.7	180.5	248.0
Provision of land and buildings	22.1	16.5	16.6	12.1	21.6	25.7
Selective assistance to industry in assisted areas	—	—	0.6	31.2	35.9	76.0
Other regional support	6.6	8.3	8.3	8.8	10.1	11.6
Regional employment premium*	212.4	192.1	161.0	156.6	191.2	215.0
Residual expenditure under repealed sections of the Local Employment Act 1972	53.0	47.1	64.9	40.0	1.7	-4.9
Scottish and Welsh Development Agencies	—	—	—	—	—	12.7
Total	294.1	264.0	262.2	358.4	441.0	584.1
Industrial Innovation						
General industrial R. and D.	32.1	29.0	28.0	30.8	32.2	36.7
Technological and industrial sponsorship	6.2	2.3	4.8	4.4	3.8	7.6
Aircraft and aero engine general R. and D. programme	14.9	14.1	18.1	19.7	19.6	17.4
Concorde—development	103.8	93.9	62.7	49.5	44.2	32.7
production	12.0	22.5	37.1	44.4	38.0	22.6
RB211	20.9	104.8	68.5	25.0	38.5	0.9
Other aircraft and aero engine projects and assistance	44.4	32.2	-2.1	39.2	26.4	113.8
Space	11.7	12.0	11.0	13.9	17.4	21.7
Nuclear	82.1	73.8	72.2	82.2	71.0	101.2
Total	328.1	384.6	307.3	309.1	291.1	354.6
General support for industry						
National Enterprise Board	—	—	—	—	—	50.0
Selective assistance to individual industries, firms, and undertakers	—	—	8.8	15.8	21.1	326.5
Promotion of tourism	10.1	17.4	24.4	42.3	18.9	16.3
Refinancing of home shipbuilding lending	—	—	78.2	135.7	115.9	94.0
Assistance to the shipbuilding industry	0.6	7.3	18.6	24.5	50.8	37.3
Other support services	34.0	-27.2	-22.2	-22.2	201.4	10.3
Investment grants	808.2	635.4	384.3	233.2	101.8	63.0
Total	852.9	632.9	487.8	429.3	509.9	597.4

	1970–71	1971–72	1972–73	1973–74	1974–75	1975–76
Support for nationalised industries (other than the transport industries)						
Compensation for price restraint	80.8	59.3	71.4	430.7	640.4	85.3
Assistance to the Coal Industry:						
Coal Industry Act	44.8	181.5	124.9	383.4	79.6	45.9
Pneumoconiosis Scheme	—	—	—	—	60.0	40.0
Other compensation	—	—	19.9	7.4	8.5	12.7
Safety and product quality and other services ...	0.6	0.9	0.9	1.0	1.0	1.3
Total	126.2	241.7	217.1	827.5	789.7	185.2
International trade						
Export promotion and trade co-operation	11.6	9.7	8.7	10.7	10.2	13.7
Refinancing of fixed rate export credits ...	—	—	501.7	545.7	528.6	458.0
Cost escalation guarantees	—	—	—	—	—	–0.8
Regulation of domestic trade and industry and consumer protection	2.4	1.1	1.5	2.0	4.2	6.9
Functioning of the labour market						
Employment services and industrial rehabilitation	44.2	47.7	54.4	61.4	57.5	86.7
Industrial training	59.9	49.2	69.9	74.3	85.8	178.8
Redundancy fund payments	73.5	97.7	66.3	42.6	51.6	97.4
Industrial relations and other labour market services ...	7.5	6.7	38.7	8.2	7.4	24.6
Total	185.1	201.3	229.3	186.5	202.3	387.5
TOTAL	1800.4	1735.3	2015.6	2482.7	2777.0	2586.6

7

There are two important points that need to be made as regards this estimate. First, it was an *underestimate* of the true extent of the subsidy morass in 1970-71, as no account was (or could be) taken of the unknown amount of subsidies hidden in public sector purchasing programmes; nor did the Denton *et al* analysis cover the full extent of the subsidy morass (e.g., it dealt mainly with government subsidies to private manufacturing industry and largely excluded an examination of government subsidies to public enterprises). Secondly, given the rapid growth of government expenditure on 'trade, industry and employment' since 1970-71, as shown in Table I, there can be no doubt that the size of the subsidy morass is very much larger today.

The 'New' Industrial Strategy: More of the Same
The central election promise of the incoming Labour government of 1974 was to "get Britain moving again" after the drop in industrial output and employment caused by the preceding miners' strike and the three-day working week. Its policies for this were unveiled initially in a White Paper published in August 1974.[5] However, following much public criticism of the course of industrial policy over the subsequent year, Mr Benn was removed from the Department of Trade and Industry, and the government's policies were further elaborated and modified in another White Paper published in November 1975.[6] These two documents are referred to by Labour government ministers as the 'new industrial strategy'.

The only thing that really *is* new about this industrial strategy is the wholeheartedness with which the economic philosophy of the corporate state has been embraced by a British government. The basis of the strategy is to 'bring together the interests of all concerned' – large companies, large trade unions, and the government – so that 'Industry and Government are explicit partners in a close relationship'. 'Regular discussions with both sides of industry' are to take place in the forums provided by state institutions such as the National Economic Development Council (NEDC), and industrial behaviour is to be aligned to 'national needs'. Henceforth, the three sides 'will work together cooperatively' in the national interest towards 'agreed national objectives'. A clearer statement of corporatist economic policy would be hard to conceive.

The primary purpose of the new industrial strategy is the "regeneration" of British industry – the encouragement of greater efficiency, dynamism, and international competitiveness. How is this laudable goal to be achieved? First, data is being collected on the past performance of industries and firms by the government and NEDC, regarding such matters as size and growth rate, external trading performance, competitiveness, interdependence with other firms/industries, import content of purchases, the general context of the growth of world demand that they face, and so on. Secondly, the implications for the future demand facing each industry of government medium-term (PESC) projections of its own behaviour are being analysed. Thirdly, the 'possibility' of new developments in each sector is being evaluated – the possibility of improvements in performance, greater import substitution, the development of new technologies, and so forth. Considerations of minimum viable size, growth of overseas competition, security of overseas materials supplies, and employment effects are included under this heading.

The purpose of the foregoing forecasting and evaluation exercise is to provide a basis for the formulation of the government measures of 'coordinated intervention and support', both at the industry and company level. Where the projected performance of either a company or an entire sector fails to conform to (largely undefined) 'government priorities' or 'national needs', then taxpayers' money is used to induce a change in performance. 'Selective financial assistance' is used to promote jobs, growth, and modernization. The National Enterprise Board – set up under the 1975 Industry Act with £1000m. of taxpayers' money at its disposal – is to promote industrial efficiency by reorganizing industry, to create jobs by investing in companies in areas of high unemployment, and to generate greater exports and more import substitution by injections of government equity capital into appropriate firms. Public purchasing policies are being used 'constructively' towards the same ends. The Manpower Services Commission is spending money to meet the 'needs' of growth sectors, and so forth.

In short, apart from its overtly corporatist ideology, there is nothing new about the new industrial strategy. It does not represent any turning away from policies of industrial subsidization. Quite the reverse: it is simply more of the same. The fundamental hypothesis of the new industrial strategy is that the efficiency and competitiveness of British industry can be regenerated by varied injections of taxpayers' money. The 'new' strategy in fact represents a formalization and extension of the pre-existing trend of British industrial policy towards greater government subsidization of industry.

The purpose of this short study is to examine the consequences, and wisdom, of this trend of policy.

The International Context

A rapidly growing permeation of industry by government subsidies is not an uniquely British phenomenon. Similar developments can be detected in the recent history of many other advanced Western economies, such as Sweden, Norway, France, Israel, Holland, Belgium, and Denmark. Only the United States and West Germany have remained relatively immune from this phenomenon (Whiting, 1976). The emergence of a subsidy morass is to be seen in the wider context as an international phenomenon. However, as with so many other types of government intervention, Britain has been one of the leaders in the field.

This study is mainly concerned with the situation in Britain but is set in the international context as there are many lessons to be drawn in Britain from experience elsewhere. Furthermore, as I shall elaborate, a reversal of the encroaching subsidy morass must not be seen as a purely domestic problem, but rather as one involving the interests of all members of the international community. As the problem is an international one, the policies designed to tackle it must, in part, be negotiated and applied at that level.

II. Rationales for Industrial Subsidies: A Critical Appraisal

Assessing the objectives of the new bewildering variety of subsidies to British industry is by no means a straightforward task. As one authoritative study of these measures has concluded:

Industrial [subsidy] policy in the United Kingdom since 1960 can only be characterised as incoherent. The basic objectives have not been clear, trade-offs between competing objectives have not been calculated in advance, the relevance of intermediate to final objectives has been obscure, and the efficiency of the methods employed have been uncertain (Denton, 1976).

The Expenditure Committee of the House of Commons likewise concluded, pointedly, that the evidence presented to it 'gives a convincing picture of the confusion of objectives' in industrial subsidy programmes (Expenditure Committee, 1971–72). The problem, however, is not simply that of mere confusion but that much of the legislation giving force to subsidy measures is worded in such a nebulous manner as to make the underlying objectives totally unclear. For instance, under Section 8 of the 1972 Industry Act, which gave powers to use £550m. of public money on industrial "assistance", the Secretary of State for Trade and Industry was given the discretion to disburse these subsidies in what he considered to be the undefined "national interest".

However, it is possible to distil the bland wordings of ministerial pronouncements and white paper officialese into some sort of coherent statement of the supposed goals of subsidization, even though it is not necessarily clear in the case of any particular measure what was the mixture and balance of the objectives involved.

These goals may be listed, in rough order of probable importance, as: the creation or preservation of jobs; the stimulation of greater investment in industry; the promotion of technological advance or industrial modernization; the attainment of greater efficiency via the restructuring of industry; the achievement of regional "balance" in the distribution of jobs and industry; the generation of exports or substitution for imports; and the sustenance of the "national interest". This list of goals can be simplified further because not all of them are independent.

First, the stimulation of investment (via implicit subsidies in the form of depreciation allowances and explicit cash grants) has not been seen as an end in itself, but as a means towards the objective of job creation. The assumption of the simplistic Keynesian model is that the level of investment expenditure is the prime determinant of the level of employment in the economy. Given the predominance of Keynesian views in the 1950s and 1960s, the encouragement of investment came to be seen as the means of attaining the more basic goal of full employment. We may, therefore, consider the case for investment subsidies as a sub-species of the case for government subsidies to promote employment. Furthermore, the emphasis on the aggregate demand effects of investment obscured the problem that a subsidy to capital expenditure alone gave rise to a "substitution effect" in the production process. That is, the subsidized input is made relatively cheaper than formerly, so encouraging a switching in the factor input-mix of business firms towards the subsidized factor and away from the use of other factors. Investment subsidies therefore promote capital-intensive projects, and have the side-effect of creating a substitution of capital for labour in the production process. This substitution effect works directly against the underlying goal of such measures: the maintenance or creation of employment. In recognition of this inherent defect emphasis has recently shifted strongly towards the giving of direct industrial subsidies for employment, and away from that of investment incentives. For these reasons I shall not consider the topic of general investment incentives any further here.

Secondly, we can group together the goals of technological modernization, restructuring and regional balance under the general heading of the "new industrial policy". The traditional goals of industrial policy in advanced Western economies have been the promotion of competition and the prevention of monopoly and restrictive practices. The "new industrial policy" is a name given by economists to a new style or orientation in industrial policy that has been evolving in a number of Western countries over the last couple of decades. The term embraces a variety of measures, such as sectoral policies, aimed at encouraging "growth" industries, particularly where these involve advanced technology, the rationalization of declining industries, the achievement of greater economies of scale via the encouragement of mergers, and the provision of assistance to those regions or sectors which are thought to be suffering from a "weak" or declining industrial base. The present government's "new industrial strategy" is of this *genre* of industrial policy.

We thus arrive at a list of four main rationales for the existent subsidy morass: job creation and preservation; the new industrial policy; the balance of payments argument; and the national interest rationale. In this Chapter, I will examine each argument separately on its own ground and, given the pre-eminence of the jobs argument for subsidization in the U.K., I devote proportionately greater attention to this topic.

THE JOBS RATIONALE

'Without doubt, the one problem above all others in provoking the growth of financial aid to industry has been unemployment' (Denton, 1976). This has to be seen against the general background to employment policy since the mid-1960s. A phenomenon of "stagflation" – a combination of high unemployment and high inflation – in the late 1960s turned into an even more alarming phenomenon of "slumpflation" – a combination of high and *rising* unemployment twinned with high and *accelerating* inflation – in the 1970s. The orthodox macro-economic analysis of the post-war period, Keynesianism, appeared as powerless to explain as to provide a remedy, for these worsening problems. Confidence in Keynesian policies of aggregate demand management has consequently waned in all Western countries. Mr Callaghan has himself denounced Keynesian demand management in an unequivocal manner:

'We used to think that you could spend your way out of a recession, and increase employment by cutting taxes and boosting government spending. I tell you, in all candour, that that option no longer exists, and that, insofar as it ever did exist, it only worked by . . . injecting bigger doses of inflation into the economy, followed by higher levels of unemployment as the next step . . . That is the history of the past 20 years.[7]

Of course, the jargon of Keynesianism is still retained to serve as a fig-leaf for the fiscal manipulation of the electorate by the government for purposes of political profit. Governments continue to indulge in the well tried practices of tax cuts/extra social welfare spending in the run-up to an election, whilst calling this 'reflation': witness the measures of November 1977, and the tax cuts of the April 1978 budget. But the truth is that most policy-makers do not retain any confidence in aggregate demand management as a genuine and long-run solution to employment problems.[8]

As confidence in Keynesian policies has waned, so governments have increasingly turned to direct job subsidies as a means of promoting or maintaining employment. For instance, the main employment subsidy programme in Britain today, the Temporary Employment Subsidy (TES), was introduced in August 1975 as an "experiment" with a budget allocation of £14m. Since then the programme has been massively expanded, and is now projected to cost approximately £400m. per annum. And TES is only the tip of the job-subsidy iceberg in the British economy today. There are also recruitment subsidies to small firms (SFES) and for the employment of youths (YES). Furthermore, a primary motivation for the large subsidies being disbursed under the 1972 and 1975 Industries Acts has been that of preserving jobs. This is most clearly so in the large *ad hoc* industrial "rescue" operations of recent years, with such firms as B L, where maintaining employment has been quoted as the main rationale of the operation. But such is the fogginess of objectives in many subsidy programmes that it is impossible to gauge whether or not they are intended primarily as a means of propping up employment. One gains the impression that this has been the main motive for the bulk of them, but it is not possible, at least in Britain, to quantify the exact volume of industrial subsidies that are implicitly job subsidies.

The rationale for the growth of job subsidies over recent years has, however, not simply been the negative one that Keynesian policies are no longer viewed as they once were. Advocates of employment subsidies have claimed that these measures (or, at least, some varieties thereof) have the wondrous ability to (a) cut unemployment, whilst simultaneously (b) reducing the rate of inflation, and (c) cutting the public sector borrowing requirement (PSBR) – the government's budget deficit. Professor Rehn of the Swedish Institute for Social Research, an internationally-influential economist, has on these grounds called upon Western governments to indulge in 'naked and shameless' extensive subsidization of jobs (Rehn, 1975), Naturally, any government is likely to be attracted to something which is reputedly capable of cutting both stagflation *and* its budget deficit. But are these miraculous claims for job subsidies really true? Let us examine the three claims in turn.

Job Subsidies and Employment

Clearly a job subsidy is capable of increasing or maintaining employment in those firms/industries so subsidized. The question, however, is whether job subsidies have a positive effect on the level of employment as a whole or whether the extra jobs in subsidized firms are purchased at the cost of jobs lost elsewhere.

"Blanket" subsidies for all jobs are, in practice, ruled out by the astronomical costs to the public purse that would be involved. Consequently, the only feasible types of employment subsidies are those of a "marginal" nature. That is, subsidies which stimulate an increment in recruitment (as with the Small Firms Subsidy and Youth Employment Subsidy) or which induce employers to retain a portion of those employees which they had planned to make redundant (as with the TES).

These marginal employment subsidies inevitably alter the structure of labour costs in the economy. They reduce the relative costs of the firms receiving subsidies, and raise the relative costs of non-subsidized firms. If subsidized firms cut their prices in line with their relative costs, consumer expenditure will be transferred from the outputs of non-subsidized firms. Even if subsidized firms do not reduce the relative prices of their products, the subsidies they receive will help them in other ways. Subsidy revenue can be used to indulge in greater sales promotion, to undertake improvements in product quality, to bring-in work previously sub-contracted to other firms, to increase dividend payments to shareholders (so that raising equity finance, and probably loans, becomes that much easier), to increase their inventories so that it will be easier for them to respond to subsequent fluctuations in demand for their products, and in other ways. In short, whether or not subsidized firms cut their prices *vis-à-vis* non-subsidized firms, their relative business situation will be enhanced, whilst conversely those of non-subsidised firms will be worsened. Putting it in the jargon of employment subsidy analysis, marginal employment subsidies, of both the job creation and preservation varieties, give rise to a "displacement effect": the retention or stimulation of employment in subsidized firms occurs at some cost of jobs displaced in non-subsidized firms. This

15

displacement effect is not necessarily immediate.

The Government is currently measuring the employment effect of job subsidies simply by counting up the number of employees being covered by such schemes, and some journalists, apparently, accept these figures uncritically.[9] Such a procedure is totally illegitimate, as it entirely ignores the loss of jobs arising from the displacement effect of job subsidies.

The Department of Employment has attempted to glean some evidence on the displacement effect of TES by carrying out a questionnaire survey of all establishments receiving TES at the end of March 1976. The firms were asked whether their increased sales had been gained at the expense of other enterprises. Only 30 per cent of establishments – though covering 45 per cent of the jobs being subsidized – replied that their sales were gained mostly at the expense of their competitors. The other 70 per cent of respondents apparently chose not to reply positively to the question. The Department of Employment itself concluded that 'it is not clear from the survey what should be assumed about the sales made by the 70 per cent of firms not identifying displacement', and also that 'the survey does not give a clear indication of the extent of output displacement elsewhere, on the extent to which this is translated into jobs lost elsewhere, or on the timing of this displacement' (Department of Employment, 1977a).

It is worth commenting, in passing, that this survey is not only totally inconclusive, but methodologically erroneous as it was carried out *only* amongst those firms receiving TES. These firms naturally have a vested interest in being coy about any displacement effects that their subsidization has given rise to. One may confidently predict that their non-subsidized competitors, whose opinions were not canvassed at all, would be likely to take a different view. An *unbiassed* estimate requires a balanced survey of both subsidized and non-subsidized firms.

As the matter stands we can only conclude that a displacement effect of job subsidies does occur, but it is impossible on the basis of the evidence presently available to state whether this entirely, or only partly, offsets the positive employment effect of job subsidies.

The advocates of job subsidies submit, however, that there is another factor at work which clinches the argument that job subsidies have a net positive effect on the level of employment: the demand multiplier effects of the subsidies. This argument is nothing but the revivification of Keynesian precepts in job subsidy clothing. The general idea is that any increase in "autonomous" expenditures in the economy (government expenditure, investment expenditure, exports) will generate a multiple rise in the levels of output and employment that is a multiple of the initial rise in autonomous expenditure, on the grounds that one man's expenditure is another man's income. A rise in any component of autonomous expenditure will thus raise income and expenditures generally, as the demand expansion ripples throughout the economy in a multiplying fashion.

It is necessary to note at this point that the simple multiplier theorems of Keynesian economic analysis work only on the basis of certain pre-suppositions. In particular, they assume that (a) the change in demand conditions initiated by the government (here, in the form of subsidy expenditures) does not alter the expectations and behaviour patterns of the non-governmental participants of the politico-economic system, and that (b) where the increased government expenditure is financed by an expansion of its deficit, then any potential side-effects of the increased deficit on output and employment can be ignored.

Neither assumption is now accepted in modern economic analysis. As regards (a), a large body of research now suggests that workers, firms, and households formulate expectations about their economic environment, including government behaviour, and adapt their behaviour accordingly. In the present context, the implication of this is that if governments start to spend extensively and in a predictable, non-random fashion on job subsidies, workers and firms will start to formulate expectations which will undermine any positive employment effect in the long run.[10] As regards (b), it is also now realized that both means of deficit finance – money creation or issue of debt by the government – are quite capable of "crowding-out" an equivalent – or even *greater* –amount of output and employment through their effects on the rate of inflation and the level of interest rates,[11] than that arising from the additional government expenditure. Proponents of employment subsidies maintain, however, that these measures actually *reduce*, or at least do not increase, the budget deficit, and thus do not give rise to crowding-out effects. This argument is examined, and challenged, later on in this Section.

In summary, the argument that job subsidies generate an unequivocal addition to the net total of employment via multiplier effects on domestic demand rests on a highly simplistic model of the economy, whose assumptions have been subjected to strong theoretical and empirical criticism in modern economic analysis.

There is but one qualification to this conclusion which deserves mention. Certain advocates of marginal job subsidies, such as Layard and Nickell (1977) – the argument is also believed to find favour with Professor Lord Kaldor – hypothesise that these measures give rise to a multiplier effect not (primarily) through the components of domestic demand, but rather through the stimulation of exports. The argument here is that job subsidies can be viewed as an implicit export subsidy. Export markets are extremely competitive, and there is some evidence to suggest that at least large exporters base the prices of their products in foreign markets on the variable costs of their production (i.e., their labour and raw material costs) alone – overhead costs (i.e., plant and equipment) being covered by the higher prices charged in domestic markets. Consequently, any marginal job subsidy will enable exporters to lower their prices on world markets and undercut their foreign competitors. Layard and Nickell calculate, on the basis of plausible cost and other assumptions, that a marginal recruitment subsidy of one-third the average industrial wage would raise British exports by 6 per cent, and generate an extra 175,000 jobs.

It may be agreed that this argument is correct, so far as it goes. It is always possible to reduce domestic unemployment by exporting it. By means of tariffs and quotas against foreign goods, by subsidies given to its exporters and, more ingenuously, by means of export subsidies disguised as a job subsidies, any country can always increase its own employment level at the expense of employment prospects elsewhere. This is not exactly a new proposition in international trade theory. But, as has also been long recognized, the validity of the proposition rests on a crucial and deeply dubious assumption. A strategy of raising domestic employment via "beggar-my-neighbour" trade distortions – whether or not this is done in the guise of job subsidies – can *only* work if other countries do not "wise up" to the attack being made on their own employment situation or, if they do, that they will not retaliate in kind. The validity of that assumption is strongly questioned in Chapter IV.

Job Subsidies and Inflation
Professor Rehn has claimed that marginal job subsidies are a vital

weapon in the fight against stagflation on the grounds that they not only produce an increase in employment but also a reduction in the rate of inflation: both elements of the stagflation problem are simultaneously dealt with. The first of these claims has been *inconclusively* analysed above; I now turn to the latter.

The "dampening effect" of job subsidies on the rate of inflation that Rehn proclaims is viewed as working through three channels (Burton, 1977a). First, job subsidies have a "direct cost-reducing effect" on the average labour costs of subsidized firms. As prices are related to costs –and labour costs are typically a large element in total costs – job subsidies may lead to price reductions, or at least a reduction to below the level at which they would otherwise have been. Secondly, job subsidies have a "capacity-utilization effect" on costs and prices. The average production costs of any establishment tend to be related to the degree of its capacity-utilization. The closer a plant runs to full capacity, the more its overhead costs can be spread over larger output runs, and the more efficient is plant utilization. By enabling firms beset by depression to work their plant closer to their capacity, job subsidies reduce their unit costs of production. Again, to the extent that the cost reduction feeds through into the firms' prices, the rate of inflation will be dampened. The third channel works on the presumption that job subsidies reduce the budget deficit. To the extent that they do so, there is less pressure on the government to finance the deficit by recourse to monetary expansion. If it is assumed that the rate of growth of the money supply is an important determinant of the rate of inflation – as much evidence seems to indicate – then job subsidies may possibly reduce the rate of inflation through this "indirect monetary effect".

The arguments regarding the first two of these three means by which job subsidies are thought to dampen inflation involve serious and basic errors of economic analysis. They rest on a simple confusion between the notions of the *level* of prices and the *rate* of inflation. A job subsidy cannot effect a permanent reduction in the rate of inflation via these two effects unless the size of the subsidy is escalated continuously in each successive period (Burton, 1977c). A job subsidy that is fixed in nominal terms (as with the TES) or as a proportion of the employee's wage will only result in a *temporary* reduction in the rate of increase in costs and prices (of subsidized firms) during its introductory period. Thereafter, the *rate of increase*

19

of costs experienced by subsidized firms will resume its old time-path. The direct cost-reducing effect and the capacity-utilization effect of a non-escalatory subsidy will only alter the *time-distribution* of cost and price increases over the duration of the subsidy programme, but will fail to achieve any reduction in the average rate of inflation measured over the same period.

In conclusion, job subsidies will only achieve a *sustained*, more-than-temporary, dampening in the rate of inflation if they can influence the fundamental forces determining it, be this trade-union wage-pushfulness or the rate of expansion of the money supply, or both. The effect of job subsidies on union wage bargaining behaviour is taken up further in Chapter IV. Here I turn to the consideration of the effect of job subsidies on the PSBR and, thereby, on the rate of growth of the money supply.

Job Subsidies and the Budget Deficit

Some protagonists of employment subsidies, such as Santosh Mukherjee, argue that these measures actually *reduce* the budget deficit. The argument rests on the point that to calculate the net cost to the Exchequer, savings to the public purse arising from a reduction in unemployment must be set against expenditures on job subsidies. These Exchequer savings arise in a number of ways. First, the volume of income and sales tax revenues and of mandatory social security contributions received by the state will rise as the volume of employees rises through subsidization. Secondly, state expenditure on unemployment benefits and related social security benefits will fall if formerly-unemployed workers are brought into work by subsidy measures.

Mukherjee's own calculations suggest that the sum of these exchequer savings, caused by bringing an average unemployed worker into employment, amount to 98–105 per cent of average male earnings in U.K. manufacturing for a single man, and 89–96 per cent in the case of a married man with two children (Mukherjee, 1976a). Rehn, working with figures for Europe as a whole, has similarly calculated that in a 'typical West European country' the transference of a worker from the category of insured unemployment to income-earning employment results in exchequer savings that are on average of the order of 80 per cent of the wage paid by the employer (Rehn, 1975, 1976). Mukherjee deduces from such calculations that:

> Public expenditure applied selectively in order to induce more employment (through *e.g.* subsidization of jobs) would not be a net burden: it would not, that is to say, increase the budget deficit further (Mukherjee, 1976a)

and:

> sizeable government outlays in keeping people in work would not increase the budget deficit but would reduce it. (Mukherjee, 1976b).

The argument is simply that if the exchequer savings are, say, 90 per cent of the average industrial wage, and the job subsidy per employee is less than 90 per cent of that wage, it will result in a net improvement (reduction) in the budget deficit: the savings will be greater than the subsidy outgoings.

Unfortunately, these deductions are on the basis of highly simplistic and fallacious reasoning. They entirely ignore the probability that there are job *losses* arising from employment subsidies which need to be set against their positive employment effects in calculating the *net* effect on the level of employment, and thus the *net* effect on exchequer receipts and disbursements. It is entirely possible that the loss of jobs arising from the displacement, crowding-out, expectations, and international trade retaliation effects of job subsidies equal their positive (covered-worker and multiplier) employment effects. In this case, the exchequer savings by bringing some workers into employment through job subsidies will simply be cancelled out by the burden to the exchequer of the jobs that have been indirectly destroyed by the subsidies. There would then be no net savings to the exchequer, and the net exchequer cost is simply equal to the gross exchequer cost. In such a case, the effect of job subsidies on the budget deficit is unambiguously positive, and equal to the gross government expenditure on the measure.

It is also possible – we do not have the detailed econometric studies that would be necessary to conclude on this matter – that the negative (displacement, etc.) employment effects of job subsidies are smaller, or *greater*, than their positive effect. Here the net effect on the budget deficit would be respectively smaller than, or *greater than*, their gross public cost. The general point is that calculations of the type carried out by Mukherjee and Rehn are erroneous because they entirely assume away, without justification, the complex side-effects of job subsidies on the level of employment.

However, even if we follow Rehn and Mukherjee in assuming away all side-effects, it is still not necessarily true that their conclusions follow from their premises. Let us assume that the negative employment effects of job subsidies just equal and offset their multiplier effects in such a way that the average duration of unemployment is left unchanged. The net employment of a job subsidy programme will then just be equal to the number of workers brought into employment by the subsidy. Even under these assumptions the Rehn-Mukherjee calculations of the effect of job subsidies on the budget deficit are incorrect, because they ignore the crucial question of the *time-duration of job subsidization relative to the time duration of worker-unemployment.* Whether or not job subsidies increase or decrease the budget deficit depends not only on the size of the subsidy relative to the size of exchequer savings,, but on the relative magnitude of these two time-periods.

To explain this point, let us assume that the size of the job subsidy per week (S) is 30 per cent of the average weekly wage (W), so that $S = 0.3W$. This approximates the situation with TES and SFES in the U.K. Let us also make use of Mukherjee's calculation that the exchequer saving per week (E) from bringing an unemployed worker into income-generating employment is approximately equal to 90 per cent of the average weekly wage, so that $E = 0.9W$. The exchequer cost (C) of the job subsidy, per subsidised worker, is then given by:

$$C = S \times d_s = 0.3W \times d_s \qquad (1)$$

where d_s is the duration of the subsidy in weeks,

The exchequer savings (V) arising from the subsidy, per subsidized worker, is likewise given by:

$$V = E \times d_u = 0.9W \times d_u \qquad (2)$$

where d_u is what would have been the average duration of unemployment in weeks of the subsidized workers had they not been covered by a job subsidy.

The net cost to the exchequer (N) – the impact on the budget deficit – is then given from equations (1) and (2) as:

$$N = C - V = 0.3W (d_s - 3d_u) \qquad (3)$$

Mukherjee, on the other hand, calculates N (incorrectly) as:

$$N = S - E \qquad (4)$$

which ignores completely the factor of the duration of subsidization relative to the duration of unemployment, and which needs to be brought into the picture.

Some concrete assumptions may here help to make things clearer. Let us assume that d_u is on average 8 weeks, and the duration of a job subsidy is 24 weeks. In this case, given our assumptions, $C = 0.3W \times 8$ and $V = 0.9W \times 24$, so that the impact of the subsidy on the budget deficit is zero. It is neither reduced nor increased by the job subsidy. If we retain our assumption that d_u is 8 weeks, but now assume that d_s is 52 weeks, then the job subsidy will *increase* the budget deficit: the cost to the exchequer of the subsidy will be twice the exchequer saving.

Given our assumptions, the crucial question thus concerns the actual sizes of d_s and d_u "in the real world". Under the TES scheme, a job subsidy of £20 p.w. per worker is claimable by employers for a period of 12 months in respect of each planned redundant worker who is retained; the firm can then apply for a further £10 p.w. subsidy per worker for a further six months.[12] The average duration of subsidization under TES is thus greater than a year. This is, of course, small beer compared to some of the more long-standing job subsidies; in some sectors of British industry or the regions, the duration of explicit or implicit subsidies to promote jobs would have to be measured in quinquennia and decades.[13]

Studies of mass redundancy suggest that d_u is likely to be far shorter than the d_s indicated above. In a study of 1,500 white-collar redundancies Wedderburn (1964) found that 48 per cent of the employees laid off found work immediately, 84 per cent within one month of leaving, and 92 per cent within two months. In another study of 1,500 redundancies resulting from the closure of the Gorton and Faverdale rail workshops, she found that 37 per cent found other work without any intervening unemployment, and 52 per cent found other work within one month. One year after the closure, only 10 per cent were still out of work – most of whom had reached (or nearly reached) retirement, or were seriously ill and/or handicapped (Wedderburn, 1965). Another study by Daniel (1972) of mass redundancy in south-east London likewise found that 39 per cent obtained other jobs prior to dismissal, and 49 per cent within one month. Only 11 per cent took more than 6 months to find another job. Mackay's (1972) study of redundancy in the West Midlands engineering industry found – *excluding those who found work immediately* – that the median duration of unemployment for the redundant workers was 8 weeks.

These studies of mass redundancy – which, being highly concentrated in time and space, tend to pose the most chronic type of unemployment problem – merely illustrate the general picture regarding the duration of unemployment: not only does a large fraction of job-changers (both of the voluntary and involuntary variety) find other work without any intervening unemployment,[14] but, even for those who do register as unemployed, the median duration of unemployment is low:

> It is clear that a *very* large part of the register (and a larger part of any group of new registrants) represents short-term turnover of persons moving from one job to another and remaining on the register for only a short time (Department of Employment and Productivity, 1968).

Wood (1975) has calculated that in the 24-year period 1948–1971 between two-thirds and two-fifths of the registered wholly unemployed in the U.K. found new work within 8 weeks. Nor has this picture of massive *short-term* turnover on the unemployment register changed as a result of the recent years of recession in the mid-1970s. As at July 1977, for instance, Department of Employment (1977b) figures show that for approximately 40 per cent of those on the register the duration of unemployment was 8 weeks or less, and for 65 per cent it was 26 weeks or less.

These comparisons, although not conclusive, suggest that the duration of subsidization tends to be many times greater in the U.K. than the likely duration of unemployment had those now covered by job subsidies not been subsidized – especially when we remember that the duration of unemployment for many job-changers is zero. If we ignore the positive and negative side-effects of job subsidies on employment – as do Rehn and Mukherjee – the strong likelihood is that job subsidies have significantly added to, rather than reduced, the budget deficit. Furthermore, once the factors discussed in Chapter IV are brought into the picture, this likelihood is greatly reinforced.

Conclusion on the Jobs Rationale
The supposedly miraculous abilities of job subsidies simultaneously to expand total employment on the one hand and cut inflation and the PSBR on the other do not stand up to critical scrutiny. This rationale is based on naive assumptions and, indeed, serious errors of analysis.

THE NEW INDUSTRIAL POLICY RATIONALE

The New Industrial Policy (NIP) is a term now being given by economists to an historically-recent orientation in the industrial policies of a number of advanced Western countries, of which the present British government's "new industrial strategy" is a, if not *the,* prime example. NIP embraces a variety of subsidy programmes and related government interventionary measures. Its central feature is the use of taxpayers' money – via subsidies, loans and government equity finance (sometimes mixed) – to promote change and "modernization" at the micro-economic level.

As with job subsidies, a major factor in the rise of NIP has partly been disillusionment with Keynesian macro-demand management as a cure for economic problems. Here, however, the emphasis is more on the failure of Keynesian measures to provide a solution for the problems of particular sectors of the economy, including both industries and regions. Macro-management techniques fail to deal with *distribution* of growth prospects and job opportunities across the economy. Boosting aggregate demand results only in the exacerbation of shortages in those sectors that are already doing well, whilst perhaps doing relatively little to solve the problems of those sectors which are struggling. The answer, it is diagnosed, lies in a shift away from macro-demand-management to a micro-interventionist, supply-side approach. This is tied in with a growing realisation that Keynesian measures provide no real solution to problems of the general level of unemployment. To this latter extent, NIP overlaps extensively, at least in the U.K., with the jobs rationale for subsidization. It is significant that one of the primary statements of the new industrial strategy by an economist (an adviser to Mr Benn) is entitled *The Economics of Labour Subsidies* (Cripps, 1976). It is thus difficult to draw an entirely clear line between the jobs and NIP rationales for industrial subsidies.

NIP sometimes is disaggregated by economists into "structural" and "sectoral" policies. "Structural" policies comprise the use of taxpayers' money to "rationalize" or restructure the organization of industry, particularly via the promotion of mergers, in order to promote greater efficiency in production. "Sectoral" policies, as the title suggests, are aimed at particular sectors of the economy, of two main sorts. First, some sectoral policies are concerned with encouraging the growth of relatively "infant" sectors: sectors that are at a lower level of development than others within the economy, or which are lagging behind (e.g., in terms of size or technology) their counterparts in other countries. Especial emphasis is commonly placed on the problems of those sectors diagnosed as being "advanced" or "high" technology industries in the latter context. Secondly, sectoral policies are aimed at rejuvenating "senile" sectors that are in (domestic) decline, especially those contracting as a result of stiffening foreign competition. "Regional" policies can be viewed in this light as a spatial application of sectoral policy, as problems of regional imbalance boil down to the existence of spatially-concentrated versions of "infant" or "senile" sector problems (or a mix of both).

The Evolution of NIP in the United Kingdom

The proximate origins of the NIP rationale for subsidization in the U.K. lie in the Labour Party's 1964 election manifesto, which promised (in Harold Wilson's words) a 'white-hot technological revolution' or, more clearly:

> a deliberate and massive effort to modernize the economy; to change its structure and to develop with all possible speed the advanced technology and the new science-based industries with which our future lies.[15]

The structural policy variant of this NIP found its first expression in the Industrial Reorganization Act of 1967. This established a state body, the Industrial Reorganization Corporation (IRC), to undertake mergers in the interests of greater efficiency. This subsequently promoted a number of mergers with taxpayers' money including the computer, ball-bearing, aircraft instrument, and car-assembly industries (British Leyland was a creation of the IRC). Although the IRC was 'expected to earn a commercial return overall on its operation' it, in fact, provided funds to private companies at way below the price on the private capital market for comparable projects. Indeed, as one major study has concluded, 'in many cases it is doubtful if the borrowers [from the IRC] would have been in a position to obtain funds from other sources at *any* interest rate' (Denton, O'Cleireacain and Ash, 1975). Subsequently disbanded by the Conservative administration of 1970–74, the IRC was replaced by the National Enterprise Board (NEB), established under the 1975 Industry Act whose purpose, like its forerunner, is laid down as the improvement of industrial efficiency via the restructuring of industrial companies and sectors. However, unlike the IRC, which did not retain any equity involvement in the products of its "restructuring" efforts, the NEB operates primarily via the purchase of equity stakes in previously private concerns, or by the provision of loan assistance in return for an equity stake. Although supposedly committed to profitability in its 'main operations', its main acquisition to date has been British Leyland. The NEB thus apparently continues in the tradition of its forerunner, the IRC, investing taxpayers' money in unprofitable projects.

Sectoral policy for "high" technology industry found its first major expression in the Development of Inventions and Science and Technology Acts of 1965.[16] The purpose of the latter was to support allegedly high risk R&D projects and diffuse benefits via government purchasing programmes, and to accelerate the introduction of technological innovations in other industries via the pre-production order scheme (whereby the government purchased pre-production equipment and lent it out free of charge). The Industrial Expansion Act of 1968 was likewise designed to 'promote efficiency; to support technical advance; or to create, expand or sustain productive capacity' via injections of taxpayers' money.[17] This Act was subsequently used to create mergers in the computer industry, to establish a primary aluminium smelter industry in Britain,[18] and to make large loans and credit guarantees for the Concorde and the QEII, amongst other things. This Act was condemned by the incoming Conservative administration of 1970 for its misuse of taxpayers' money; but only two years later, this administration itself produced a sectoral policy in the form of the 1972 Industry Act. This provided for selective (as well as general) government subsidies for the purpose of job creation and modernization in the regions and individual industries, as well as in the undefined 'national interest'. The 1972 Act has now become a major vehicle for the prosecution of sectoral policy under the present Labour Government's "new" industrial strategy. Large subsidies are currently being provided under a motley of sectorally-"tailored" packages of subsidy money to the electronic components, machine tools, clothing, ferrous foundry, non-ferrous foundry, poultrymeat processing, redmeat slaughterhouses, textile machinery, paper and board, printing machinery and wool textiles industries. More than £250m. of taxpayers' money has been currently allocated to this clutch of sectoral subsidy schemes, which are estimated to pay for about one-fifth of the average project costs of the industrial projects so subsidized.

Regional policy has a longer history in the U.K. than the foregoing structural and sectoral policies towards industry, but has become increasingly related to these policies, as part of an overall NIP package. Thus, for instance, the motivation behind the subsidies given to the shipbuilding and primary aluminium smelting industries, and those granted under the 1972 Industry Act, have had a strong regional element to them. "Regional" policy measures have now become so extensive that the greater part of the surface area of the U.K. is now eligible for regional subsidies of one sort and another; indeed, the complex of subsidies available under this head are now so numerous that it takes a 44-page booklet just to list them (Department of Industry, 1976).[19] Simultaneous subsidies can in fact be received under a variety of regional schemes; the total of such assistance often adding up to three quarters of the outlay on set-up costs in the "assisted" areas.

The Arguments for NIP

The justification for NIP in terms of economic analysis is obscure. As one economist who is an advocate of industrial subsidies on this account has conceded, 'the case for government [NIP] intervention in industry cannot readily be understood in terms of traditional economic analysis of the market economy' (Cripps, 1976). Nor have such advocates yet provided any new and well-developed economic theory that does so provide a sound analytical foundation for NIP.

To the extent that the NIP "rationale" for subsidies derives from any sort of intellectual foundation at all, it rests on *ad hoc* assertions concerning the existence of "market imperfections" which, it is argued, require government subsidies to "correct" the workings of the market. The main variants of this claim are described below.

(1) The "Excessive Caution" Argument. Private enterprises are too cautious in undertaking investment in infant industries that promise to be prodigies and senile industries that are in need of rejuvenation in one form or another. The government must step in with subsidy inducements to overcome this "excessive" caution in business behaviour.

(2) The "Externalities" Argument. Firms base their business decisions on the expected "private" costs and benefits of their actions, that is, the costs and benefits to the firm itself. Consequently, they ignore "external" or "social" costs and benefits

that their investment, location, actions etc. give rise to. Government intervention – via subsidies, taxes, or regulatory measures – is therefore necessary to adjust the allocation of resources in a socially-optimal fashion. This argument has been used to justify a myriad of interventionary measures, running from nationalization, fishing policy, and the prevention of competition to the maintenance of uneconomic branch railway lines. In the field of industrial subsidies, two major sub-species of this argument are commonly found:

(a) *The "Spin-Off" or "Fall-Out" Argument* – The innovations made in "advanced technology" industries often have diffuse applications in other industries. Advanced technology firms will not take these diffuse external benefits into account in the R&D investment decisions. Subsidies are necessary in these industries to avoid under-investment in such R&D work.

(b) *The "Social Costs of Unemployment" Argument* – Contracting firms fail to take account of the social costs of unemployment that their run-down gives rise to.

(3) The *"Investment Funds Insufficiency" Argument*. Certain investment programmes are so large in scale that the funds necessary to undertake them are unavailable from private sources. The scale of these projects necessitates government funding. This argument is applied especially to advanced technology industries, where the overhead costs of R&D work, pilot projects and production line set-up costs may run into £billions. New jetliners, such as the Concorde, serve as an example.

(4) *The "Myopia" Argument*. Private investors and business firms are "short-sighted" in evaluating investment projects that will generate returns over a very long time span. In the jargon of economics, they discount the future returns on investment at a rate which is higher than the socially-optimal discount rate. Government action (e.g., subsidies) is necessary to induce business firms to overcome this myopia.

(5) *The "Imperfect Capital Market" Argument*. Not all firms find it possible to raise the funds they need for investment on the capital market. "Gaps" exist in the provision of funds to industry by the capital market, which government has to fill with taxpayers' money (this argument is a generalization of (3) above). One of the white

papers detailing the present U.K. government's new industrial strategy, for instance, speaks of 'imperfections in the capital markets mainly at the medium- and longer-term ends', and of 'a capital market which does not give priority to the needs of industry'.[20]

(6) *The "Economies-of-scale" Argument.* Firms in both "infant" and "senile" industries would operate at lower cost and higher profits if they could expand and take advantage of economies of scale. Government action – in the form of subsidy-lubricated mergers, "rationalization" and restructuring – is necessary to allow such firms to reap these potential scale economies.

(7) *The "Cumulative Spiral" Argument.* This argument has been briefly put by Francis Cripps:

> In many industries the long-run prospects of individual firms tend to improve or worsen with cumulative effects. Initial success provides the opportunities for exploiting economies of scale and specialization, together with the profit and easy access to external finance needed to fund continual expansion. In this situation continued productivity improvements will follow as a result of growth from an initially advantageous position. On the other hand, initial failure results in continued slow growth, lack of finance, inability to reorganise and low productivity growth.
>
> This analysis provides a justification for any form of subsidy which is sufficient to set a firm or industry on the path of sustained expansion. It is an argument for selective, temporary subsidies to rescue industrial invalids and restore them to health – after which they should be able to survive and prosper without further aid. (Cripps, 1976).

(8) *The "Labour Immobility" Argument.* There is evidence that labour is highly immobile between regional sectors and, to a lesser extent, between occupations. 'Redundant workers appear remarkably reluctant to move to jobs outside their home and travel-to-work area . . . it is thus entirely rational for policy to attempt to encourage the provision of new jobs by investment in those locations where old jobs are being depleted most quickly . . . the . . . argument for such regional policy [is] the social one of giving recognition to locational preference' (Greenwood, 1977).

(9) *The "Wage Rigidities" Argument.* "Institutional" factors produce uniform wage rise in different sectors, despite sectoral variations in demand conditions. Therefore, wages in sectors facing demand contraction cannot adjust to the level which would sustain employment levels in those sectors, and "structural" unemployment emerges. (A factor often singled out in this regard is industry-wide collective bargaining, so that wage rates negotiated at the national

level, and applied uniformly across the country, produce unemployment in certain regions). Government action in the form of regional/selective industrial assistance is therefore necessary to mop up the structural unemployment so caused.

These, then, constitute the main arguments in the NIP rationale for government subsidization and other measures of government intervention in industry. But do they stand up to close inspection?

The Arguments Examined

Let us examine these nine arguments in turn.

(1) *The 'Excessive Caution' Argument.* It is certainly an observable, indeed commonplace, fact that people tend to be more cautious when allocating their own resources than when they are allocating somebody else's, especially if the latter is unknown to them. In particular, individuals tend to be notably more cautious in making decisions that will directly affect their own wealth or job prospects than are vote-gathering politicians and tenured civil servants notionally acting "on the behalf" of the public. The reason is simple: The structure of incentives facing the two groups differs. The former provides strong incentives to choose carefully and to avoid mistakes; the individual's own economic welfare is directly involved; he will bear the costs of any mistaken judgment, and will directly gain from a sound judgment. Politicians and bureaucrats allocating taxpayers' money, on the other hand, have considerably reduced economic incentives to act in such a careful manner. It is a plain fact that political and bureaucratic decision-makers can make rash decisions or bad mistakes involving possibly hundreds of £ millions of public funds and bear absolutely no personal cost whatsoever. Nor can they reap any of the pecuniary benefits of a financially sound investment. There may, of course, be some political comeback from an unprofitable allocation of taxpayers' money; but this acts as a very weak incentive mechanism. First, only a few such cases come to public light, let alone become well-known amongst the electorate. Secondly, even in the case of those mistaken decisions that do come to light, the prospect of job loss for the ministers and bureaucrats involved is apparently very slight.

The point here is not a party political one at all. The point is about the structure of incentives facing private decision-makers on the one hand and political and bureaucratic decision-makers on the other. It is a *prediction of economic analysis* that, given these

31

differential incentive structures, we should expect to find that greater caution is displayed in avoiding losses by private as against public decision-makers. The evidence available provides ample confirmation of that prediction.

It is thus most curious, not to say paradoxical, that this argument has been used as an attempt to *justify* government subsidization. The clear implications for public policy are precisely to the contrary! Fewer resourses are likely to be wasted on unprofitable, inefficient activities if government subsidization of industry does not occur.

(2) *The "Externalities" Argument.* This argument for government intervention has been shown to be deeply flawed, by recent developments in the economic analysis of property rights and related topics. The full problems cannot be reviewed here,[21] but a central, and commonsense, point is that government action to correct externalities is not costless, and the cost may outweigh the supposed social benefits to be gained. For instance, aircraft launching aid involved a net subsidy of £1,300m. (at 1974 prices) over the period 1945–1975. But studies of the aircraft industry have had great difficulty in finding genuine social benefits from aircraft production that would offset any but the merest fraction of that heavy cost to the taxpayer (Gardner, 1976; Hartley, 1975). The "spin-off" or "fall-out" argument for subsidising advanced technology industries is especially weak, as these studies suggest. Indeed, the very argument is based on fallacious reasoning. Firms – whether in high technology industries or otherwise – will only fail to take into account the spin-off from their innovations if they cannot fully appropriate the returns from the spin-off. Of course, other firms may seek to steal valuable industrial information – which will impair the returns to the innovating firm. But the problem of theft is not peculiar to industrial information: it is 'a situation which applies to any valuable asset' (Hartley, 1975). It is true, however, that the law against theft gives less adequate protection to intellectual property than it does to material possessions. The answer to this, however, lies not in subsidies but in a reinforcement and updating of the law.

The social costs of unemployment argument for subsidizing declining sectors is also fallacious. These costs are not social or external costs in the proper technical sense in which these terms are used within economics. In the proper sense of the term, a social or external cost is one which cannot be "internalized" by negotiation between the parties to the effect, due to technical factors or attenuations in property rights that prevent such trades from taking place. Employees faced with a reduction in demand for their services in the sector in which they are currently working can, in principle, always avoid the costs of job change and potential unemployment by trading with their current employers – that is, by offering to work at reduced wage rates. Whether they prefer to move or to stay (at lower wages) the employees are probably going to suffer a real income loss. But this is *not* the same thing as an externality. The market is here producing the *right* "signals": demand for the firm's/sector's products have fallen, and incentives must be created for factors of production to move into other sectors, where demand has risen. If governments shore up declining firms and industries by subsidies, then these market "signals" are destroyed (or at least weakened), and an inefficient pattern of resource allocation will result.

Of course, no one likes to lose his job or suffer a decline in his income, as a result of the evolution in the pattern of consumer demand. But this is an argument for unemployment and retraining *insurance*, not an argument for selective government assistance to senile industries on the fallacious grounds that the market is functioning incorrectly due to the presence of externalities.

(3) *The "Investment Funds Insufficiency" Argument.* This is simply an "armchair" surmise that fails to square with the facts. Capital can always be raised – *provided* the anticipated returns are sufficiently attractive. For example, the single greatest arena for investment in the U.K. over recent years has been the North Sea Oil industry. By 1976 nearly £1,800m. *per annum* of capital expenditure were being undertaken by private enterprises in the British sector alone. As this example shows, large investment projects clearly do not *require* government funding. It is large investment projects, such as the Concorde, which are anticipated to yield low or negative expected profits which have difficulty getting off the ground without government subsidies.

(4) *The "Myopia" Argument.* This again is a most muddle-headed argument. Private decision-makers have every incentive to take the future pay-offs of their investment plans into account in their present decision-making – they are the ones who will, after all, collect these pay-offs. Political decision-makers do not collect any such long-run

pecuniary benefits, and are therefore less likely to take them into account in making subsidy decisions. There is a considerable incentive for them, however, to take into account the *short-run political* benefits of avoiding the run-down of senescent firms and industries. Votes can be bought by subsidies, or at least, not lost, in the constituencies where such enterprises are concentrated. Both factors conspire to produce a serious economic myopia in government decision-making compared to private decision-making. As Head of the Government Economic Service from 1964 to 1969, Sir Alec Cairncross was exceedingly well placed to observe this phenomenon:

> In democratic society governments have an uncertain length of life and hesitate to curtail it deliberately by giving precedence to long-run gains at the cost of short-term unpopularity . . .
>
> Economic myopia of this kind does not, however, deter governments from taking large risks [for the economy] with considerable light-heartedness. For they may enter into commitments involving heavy eventual outlays so long as they either win immediate credit or escape from awkward political dilemmas or gratify some critical section of opinion.

(Cairncross, 1970)

(5) *The "Imperfect Capital Market" Argument.* This argument has been disposed of by Professor Stigler of Chicago University. As he notes,

> The most pervasive imperfection-in-the-capital-market is the inability to borrow funds . . .
>
> The demonstration of this imperfection invariably consists in the high rates of interest earned or paid by the investor. Yet, this is surely not sufficient evidence to allow us to conclude that capital is being allocated inefficiently – any more than the fact that some people walk is proof of an imperfection in the automobile market. (Stigler, 1967).

Of course not all firms can get the investment funds they "need" – *at a price they are willing to pay.* This is not to deny that the supply of savings would be much greater, and the level of interest rates much lower, if (a) the government did not continue to borrow massive volumes of savings to fund its budget deficit, and (b) taxation did not impinge so heavily on the activity of saving in Britain.

(6) *The "Economies-of-Scale" Argument.* The "analysis" underlying this argument is most curious. If the achievement of greater size by internal expansion or merger with other firms is expected to yield greater profits, then the owners of business firms have every incentive to undertake such actions. No subsidy

34

inducements, or fiddling about by the NEB, is necessary to procure them. The case for "restructuring" lubricated by subsidies must therefore rest on either the argument that government ministers have, or have via the civil service, better information about potential economies of scale than businessmen and investors with detailed knowledge of the industry concerned, or it is 'predicated on the belief that firms will not be operated in their owners' interests' (Hindley, 1970).

One does not have to make much mention of British Leyland or the abysmal record of Whitehall control of the nationalized industries to knock down the first of these alternatives. Plainly neither government ministers nor the civil service advisers have the detailed micro-knowledge, or the incentives to acquire it, of businessmen, executives, and investors in any particular firm or industry. The second fall-back argument rests on the Galbraithian diagnosis of divorce between (the interests of) owners and controllers (managers) of large corporations. The managers of such enterprises, it is argued, are likely to pursue goals other than those of their shareholders (i.e., maximum profitability). But here the argument gets itself into tangles, because the Galbraithian argument is that the goal which the corporation managers are most likely to pursue is that of corporate size (on which their own status, power and prestige rests). In other words, they are likely to *over-expand* their corporations, beyond the point of maximum profitability. Thus, *if* the Galbraithian "divorce" argument is correct, it hardly provides a rationale for government to step in with subsidies to encourage even larger-sized companies. This would only exacerbate inefficiency.

Furthermore, the Galbraithian argument itself suffers from a defect. The market system has a built-in mechanism for checking any such Galbraithian tendencies, in the form of the market for corporate control. If the corporate managers reduce profitability by over-expansion or other acts of self-aggrandisement, the current shareholders will seek to reduce their equity holdings and find more profitable outlets for their savings. The share prices of inefficiently managed and low profit companies therefore come under selling pressure. This makes it both more difficult for the corporation to obtain equity and loan finance, and increases the prospect of a take-over bid and job loss for the incumbent management.

(7) *The 'Cumulative Spiral' Argument.* This suffers from the same general defect as the "Economies-of-Scale" argument. It ignores the role of *expected* profits. Where there is the expectation that there are sufficient profits to be made from the overcoming of barriers to expansion, or the arrest of temporary decline by reorganization, then there is every incentive to undertake changes. Where this condition is not met, such changes, of course, do not take place. Indeed, if this were not true, then no small firm would ever grow large, and no firm beset by a temporary demand contraction or other problems would ever be able to overcome it – it would simply go on plummetting down in contraction. Clearly, this is not so. Furthermore,

> If industrial invalids restored to health are supposed to survive and prosper without further aid, why are subsidies required: why not loans? (Hartley, 1976).

Indeed, why are *government* loans necessary? If the future health of the invalids is so blindingly obvious, why cannot loans be raised on private capital markets? The only answers to this question quoted by the advocates of subsidies lie in the reiteration of arguments (1), (4) or (5) –which have already been rebutted.

(8) *The "Labour Immobility" Argument.* Labour immobility in and of itself would not cause unemployment. Provided that wages are flexible then demand contraction would simply cause relative wages to fall in the affected regions, not unemployment to emerge. Secondly, it is difficult to see why it should be a goal of public policy, as expressed by Greenwood (1977), to subsidize the locational preferences of anyone at all. I have a strong locational preference for areas with a sunny climate, warm seas, and an attractive coastline. I do not, however, feel it proper to argue that other British taxpayers should buy me a villa on the Mediterranean. Likewise, if other individuals have different locational preferences, they must expect to bear the costs of those preferences.

The provision of transfer payments to people who are genuinely poor due to family circumstances and/or the inherent uncertainties of life is certainly a valid goal of public policy. But let us not confuse that valid goal with the ridiculous notion of the subsidization of locational preferences. Indeed, such a policy is likely to be counter-productive. If individuals do have strong locational preferences then subsidising those preferences will make them even *less* willing to move, and will make the problem of economic adjustment even more difficult. A more useful approach would be to reduce the costs of moving that result from government intervention (e.g., rent controls, council housing lists) in the housing market, and monopolistic make-work practices in those professions dealing with the purchase and sale of houses.

(9) *The "Wage Rigidity" Argument.* To the extent that industry-wide collective bargaining does result in regional unemployment, it would be folly to subsidize in order to offset those effects. If trade unions follow inflexible wage rate policies whatever the sectoral demand conditions, then they must expect to price some of their own members out of jobs. If government subsidies are used to mop up the unemployment so caused then, of course, trade unions have no incentive to take this effect into account in their wage bargaining policy. The subsidies merely encourage the very inflexibility that they are supposed to offset. A more useful approach would be to encourage greater decentralization in collective bargaining, so that the wage structure provided a closer fit to the specific conditions pertaining in each sector.

Conclusion on the NIP Rationale

The arguments for industrial subsidies coming under the NIP rationale fail to sustain critical examination. It is difficult to avoid concluding with Professor Ohlin (1969) that the new industrial policy lacks 'intellectual coherence'.

THE BALANCE OF PAYMENTS RATIONALE

The balance of payments (BOP) was the sacred cow of British economic policy throughout the post-war period under the era of fixed exchange rates that lasted until the early years of the 1970s, and still exerts much, if lesser, influence on the discussion of public policy today. It has come to provide 'a case for or against almost anything, and . . . distorts discussion of public policy to an absurd extent' (Hindley, 1970).

In this guise the BOP has provided a flimsy rationale or part-rationale for numerous industrial subsidy measures in the U.K. A main purpose of the 1968 Industrial Expansion Act was apparently that the 'selective and timely' use of the subsidy powers incorporated in it would help take advantage of the 1967 devaluation.[22] The BOP has also been quoted as a rationale for subsidies in the shipbuilding, aircraft, and primary aluminium industries, amongst others. In some cases the aim has been to encourage exports, in others to encourage import substitution; sometimes, both.

Such subsidy measures are in part a testimony to the alarming historical staying-power of simple mercantilist reasoning: exports are "good", imports "bad". Exports and import-substitutes should, therefore, be encouraged – by subsidies and other measures.

Such reasoning is fallacious. the promotion of high-cost import substitutes – which could have been produced more cheaply abroad – certainly increases the welfare of those in the subsidized industry, but harms the economic welfare of the general domestic taxpayer, who bears the financial cost of the subsidies, and also foreign producers, whose markets are reduced. Export subsidies, on the other hand (as in the Polish ships "deal") benefit foreign purchasers and the domestic subsidised industry, again at the cost of the domestic taxpayer. And both types of subsidies are highly likely to give rise to retaliatory measures in other countries – with the net effect that absolutely everyone is made worse off.

Subsidies are a highly inefficient means of dealing with a balance-of-payments deficit, distorting relative prices and reducing the gains from international trade. The appropriate, most direct and the cheapest means of curing a balance-of-payments deficit is simply to let market forces follow their course on the foreign exchange market. That is, the exchange rate should be allowed to find its own level, at which the demand and supply for the £ on the foreign exchange market are brought into equality.

THE NATIONAL INTEREST RATIONALE

Considerations of the "national interest" have been mentioned in respect of subsidies given to a number of British industries, such as aircraft and computers. Insofar as the "national interest" rationale has any independent identity from the other rationales for subsidization, it boils down to two separable arguments – considerations of national prestige, and national security.

National prestige considerations have been used as an argument to subsidize high-technology industries and projects, such as the development of the Concorde supersonic jetliner (Jewkes, 1972), the general presumption being that national status depends on spectacular successes in technology. But clearly this in an incorrect assumption. For the countries which have the highest prestige today are probably the United States, West Germany, Japan and Switzerland. And their reputation rests not on government-subsidized domestic industries, high-technology or otherwise, but on their general high level of efficiency, and rate of economic progress, of their economic systems. It is *economic* efficiency in *economic* performance, not *technical* expertise *per se*, which is the key to maintaining the regard of other nations. Indeed, it may be that the production of technological achievements which are economic flops – such as the Concorde – impairs rather than increases a country's ranking on the league-table of national prestige.

Considerations of the national security have also been used to justify selective subsidies to certain "strategic" industries. The Ministry of Technology argued in 1971 that a British computer industry should get government assistance, on the grounds that:

> to fail to produce an indigenous industry would expose the country to the possibilities that industrial, commercial, strategic and political decisions made in America could heavily influence our ability to manufacture, to trade, to govern, or to defend . . .[23]

The maintenance of national security is certainly a valid, indeed *basic*, objective of any nation-state. But the real question to be asked is whether selective subsidies to industry are the appropriate means of achieving this end. The first and fundamental requirement to be observed if national security is to be maintained is that we have sufficient military power to defend and deter against external attack. There is, bluntly, no point at all in subsidizing strategic industries if our armed forces are so small that they could be overrun in the space of weeks or months by a Warsaw Pact attack on Western Europe. The policy implications of the national security goal are that the nation's armed forces must have defensive and deterrent credibility. No amount of selective industrial assistance will promote national security if that basic requirement is not met.

A subsidiary requirement is, of course, that the country has reliable sources of "strategic" goods necessary to the maintenance of a credible defensive deterrent capability. But the likelihood that U.S. computer firms will refuse to sell their wares to Britain, or the U.S. government will prohibit them from doing so, is extremely improbable, requiring outlandish assumptions about the future course of developments in the U.S. and its relations with one of its closest allies.

GENERAL CONCLUSION

The supposed rationales of industrial subsidy measures appear, on detailed examination, as very weak reeds, if not entirely erroneous. As one senior Treasury official has commented:

> . . . one is left wondering more and more why, if their effects are so uncertain, so much ingenuity goes into devising new suggestions for using even more scarce public money in this way (Byatt, 1976).

The next Chapter seeks to provide an answer to that most pertinent question.

III. The Political Economy of the Subsidy Morass

If the genuine benefit/cost ratio of industrial subsidies to society is so unclear and disputable – *ignoring* the long-term dangers to be examined in Chapter IV – why *do* many governments increasingly embroil themselves in such measures?

Government Motivation, Political Bias and Encroaching Subsidization

Advocates of subsidy measures base their general argument on the existence of certain alleged "failures" or "imperfections" in the workings of the market system. The conclusion that is drawn is that, in these circumstances, government must step in with subsidies to cure these defects. The implicit assumption of this argument is that politicians and bureaucrats are economic eunuchs who have no motive other than that of acting in the "public interest".

Such a view of political behaviour is quite unrealistic. The political decision-making mechanism has its own "failures" and "imperfections". To analyse the alleged imperfections of the market without analysing the imperfections of the proposed solution is no sort of analysis at all. Indeed, it is particularly dangerous in this instance, because *democratic political systems contain an inherent bias towards subsidization of industry.* Unrealistic analysis that legitimises government subsidization thus has the unfortunate effect of unleashing these biases further.

This bias or imperfection of the democratic political system arises from a number of sources. Primarily, governments are not motiveless economic eunuchs. Economists are now finding that a useful hypothesis in the prediction of government behaviour is that they choose amongst alternative policy actions in order to maximise their voter support.[24] That is, a strong, if not dominant, motive in government behaviour is the winning of elections, for two reasons. First, political power, income and prestige and perquisites – all of which give direct utility to the politician – depend upon the retention of governance. Secondly, a political party is unable to put *any* of its desired policies into operation unless it can win a general election and form a government. There is thus a strong incentive for any government (or political party that is competing for office) to 'trim' its policies so as to maximise its probable support. This does not mean that 'the choice of policy variables which may be termed "idealistic" and which are derived from the political philosophy of the party in power are . . . precluded, but their relevance to policy action will at least be subject to the overriding constraint of retaining power by vote-getting' (Peacock, 1977).

This political concern with the retention of voter support provides an especially strong incentive for governments to undertake actions which –although they lead to economic inefficiency and/or a waste of public funds – sustain voter support in those marginal constituencies which may be decisive to the outcome of an election. Professor Prest provides an example of how such incentives bias political choice, in this case 'the economically nonsensical act . . . [of] the subsidy payments to the Central Wales railway line':

> It is reported that in the course of the 1964 to 1970 Labour government the then Ministry of Transport put forward to the Cabinet what was thought to be a cast-iron case for closure. The proposals were immediately rejected on the grounds that the line ran through six marginal constituencies. Rumour has it that it would in fact be cheaper to hire taxis for the few people who use the line. (Prest, 1976).

The same incentives are at work in the case of industrial subsidy decisions. Change is continuously going on within the market economy, in the form of technical innovation and industrial obsolescence, the emergence of new and more efficient overseas competitors, the birth and death of firms and adaptation in the industrial structure to the evolving pattern of consumer demand, material costs, and so forth. This process of economic change provides general and pervasive benefits to all members of society, as witnessed in the gradual, long-term rise in real standards of living that has occurred over the past 200 years. But change also imposes some short-term costs or losses on those in declining sectors of the economy which, moreover, are often geographically concentrated. Lobbying pressure inevitably emerges from these sectors for the government to step in with taxpayers' money to avert the decline and the short-term costs.

Reinforcing Factors

This political incentive towards subsidization – at the direct expense of the taxpayer and the long-term standard of living of society as a whole – is strongly reinforced by a number of other factors. First, given the crucial importance of winning general elections, and the relative brevity of time until the next election (maximum five years), governments have a considerable incentive to focus their attention on the short-run political pay-offs of subsidy disbursements, and to discount heavily the long-term gains to the community as a whole of allowing economic adjustments to take place. As Professor Peacock notes,

> the time horizon of politicians being usually short [and] given the assessment of ways in which voters' support might be maximised, an industrial strategy must appear to be offering immediate benefits to the community, and with unemployment dominating the short-term situation, Ministers may be under strong pressure to seek out measures which will preserve jobs in the short term . . . (Peacock, 1977).

Secondly, the proclivity of vote-maximising democratic governments towards subsidization of struggling industrial sectors is reinforced by the existence of what the Italian nineteenth-century economist Amilcare Puviani termed as the 'fiscal illusion' of the members of the tax-paying community.[25] The benefits of industrial subsidies are concentrated in time and population. No one wants to lose his present job, or to sustain a capital loss on his equity holdings, in a sector that is facing falling demand. The maintenance of firms and jobs through subsidies thus tends to be warmly applauded by this minority that benefit from the subsidies. The costs of such measures, however, are widely dispersed over both time and population. The direct fiscal costs are spread over the whole tax-paying community, and are hidden amongst a vast array of other government spending programmes, which the taxpayer is called to finance via general taxation. The tax "price" of subsidy decisions is thus unlikely to be fully perceived by the community and voter resistance to subsidy measures is therefore weakened by the existence of fiscal illusion. And the evidence suggests that there is a considerable degree of fiscal illusion amongst taxpayers.

As Puviani realised, this tendency to fiscal illusion is likely to be strongly magnified when governments have recourse to deficit finance; that is, the facility for financing public expenditure by expanding the money-supply (money creation) or by borrowing from the public (debt issue). The costs of these two forms of public finance are even more hidden from the taxpayer than are the costs of tax-financed expenditure. The cost of money creation is inflation – which functions as a hidden tax on the holding of money balances – and the economic distortions and loss of output and employment – that a variable inflation gives rise to. The cost of debt issue by the government falls on the taxpayer *in the future*, whilst raising the level of interest rates – so crowding out other borrowing for business investment in the capital market – in the short run. In both cases, the costs are separated in time from the benefits of governments spending, and are not clearly perceived as the result of government actions by members of the electorate. Fiscal systems – as in Britain today – which permit vote-maximising governments to run perpetual budget deficits are thus likely to reinforce the bias of democratic political systems towards growing government subsidization of industry.[26]

Finally, the bias of democratic politics towards industrial subsidies is reinforced by the tendency of government to favour producer interest groups (firms, unions) at the expense of consumer interests.[27] The former has greater incentive to lobby government than the latter, 'since most men earn their incomes in one activity but spend in many, the area of earning (producing) is much more vital to them than the area of spending (consuming)' (Hartley, 1975). Furthermore, it is easier for producer interest groups to organize lobbying activity than consumers as they have the resources and are existing, powerful organizations. Consumers and taxpayers neither have such resources available, nor the organization through which to mount such campaigns.

On the basis of the same economic analysis, we may predict that it is the larger, more concentrated, and more organized producer interest groups that are likely to be favoured in government subsidy (and other) decisions, than smaller, less concentrated, and less well-organized producer groups. The political significance (in terms of lobbying pressure and the threat of lost votes) of, say, 100,000 redundancies spread over 10,000 small firms in 100 constituencies is thus far less than the same number of redundancies located in, say, four large enterprises in just three constituencies. Predictably, it is the latter sort of situation that engenders the bulk of government "assistance" to industry. The history of recent British industrial subsidies clearly confirms this prediction. The subsidies going to British Leyland, British Steel, Chrysler and so forth are many thousands of times larger than the total allocation for the Small Firms Employment Subsidy.

A further complication of this political bias arises from the fact that large firm size tends to be correlated (in both the private and public sectors of industry) with the capital-intensity of production: large firms tend to be those where the ratio of capital costs to labour costs is very high. From this fact arises what might be called the "Drax B Phenomenon" in industrial subsidization: staggering amounts of taxpayers' money, running to many hundreds of £m. have to be pumped into large but ailing capital-intensive firms to avert the disappearance of a few thousand jobs – at Heaven knows what cost to jobs displaced or crowded out elsewhere in more labour-intensive firms and industries.

Conclusion

The biases embedded in the democratic political system produce a tendency towards growing government subsidization of industry – a tendency that has little or nothing to do with the genuine interests of the community as a whole, but which has much to do with the vote-maximising interests of governments, and the disproportionate influence exerted by vested producer interest groups on governmental decision-making.

This is not an argument against democracy. As Winston Churchill argued, democracy is the worst of political systems – except for all the others. It is, however, an argument for greater awareness amongst the electorate of the biases of the political system, and against which they need to be perpetually on guard. It is to be hoped that this short study contributes to that greater awareness.

IV. The Consequences of Continued Encroachment

As earlier emphasized, the emergence of the subsidy morass is an historically-recent and rapidly-growing phenomenon. It is unlikely that full adjustment has yet taken place to this new and novel set of affairs in domestic and international economic and political systems – even though the signs are already abundant that such adjustments are taking place.

This Chapter explores the question: what changes in the workings of the economy and policy are likely to take place in the long run if government subsidisation of industry continues as extensively as it is now, if not further? It is pertinent to note that the advocates of industrial subsidy measures have, without exception, failed to examine this crucial question of the long-term results of the subsidy morass.

The Long-Term Effects on Business Behaviour

Privately-owned enterprises, whether they be a one-man firm or a large multinational corporation, always seek to earn profits. In a purely market economy, in which no government subsidies exist, they are compelled to do this by producing goods and/or services that consumers are willing to pay for. Revenue can only be gained by producing and selling, and profits can be made only by finding and producing those products which (a) the consumer evaluates as being worth more to him or her than alternative uses of the expenditure involved, and (b) do not cost more to produce than they yield in revenue to the firm. In such a pure market environment, the enterprise is led by the imperative of profits to focus its attentions on the production of what the consumer is willing to pay for.

But once an extensive morass of government subsidies to industry exists, and profit-seeking enterprises have come to fully recognize the implications of this situation, the picture is radically altered. There are then two routes whereby firms can generate revenue and profits – by competition in markets for consumer expenditure, and/or by competition in lobbying for government subsidies. A clear danger, once the extent of government subsidization becomes both extensive and fully recognized, is that many exterprises may find that there are better or easier profits to be made from adroit competition for, and manipulation of, industrial subsidy programmes, than there are to be had from the hard slog of winning custom by competition in the market. All firms, in some degree, will now have an incentive to increase the amount of organizational effort that they devote to political lobbying, and conversely to reduce that devoted to production and market competition.

This prediction is no idle surmise. Corroboratory evidence for it comes from a detailed case-study of the Israeli experience of government subsidization of industry over recent decades (Finger, 1974). This study is of especial relevance to Britain because the Israeli experience, which generally preceded the development of the same phenomenon in Britain, provides one of the foremost post-war examples of growing industrial subsidization. In fact by 1967 the total of government grants and loans to manufacturing industry in Israel had surpassed that of private equity investment as a source of finance.

Professor Finger's study documents the long-term results of this situation. It finds that a class of "subsidy-maximising" firms emerged in Israel, which generated profits by the 'manipulation of subsidy systems, and whose goal is the optimization of subsidy returns'. These firms depended for their existence not on their ability to compete effectively for consumer expenditure in the market, but on their ability to compete for subsidy revenue by considerable and sophisticated lobbying of the government and the array of agencies set up by government to administer its numerous industrial subsidy programmes.

The study also details the emergence of a new class of managers, investment consultants and fiscal accountants in Israeli industry and commerce, linked to the subsidy morass. The main qualification of the members of this new class of businessmen was not their ability to produce the goods and services that customers wanted, at a price they were willing to pay, but their demonstrated ability to milk to the full the vast array of subsidies potentially available to

48

companies. Many of these new-type managers, consultants and board directors were themselves ex-members of the cadre of government officials and bureaucrats involved in the administration of industrial subsidy programmes.[28]

The economic inefficiency of such a state of affairs is obvious. First, the productivity of executives of, and consultants to, subsidy-maximising concerns comes to be measured not by the ability to generate profits for the firm by able entrepreneurship in the market, but by the number, frequency, and closeness of contacts with important government officials and bureaucrats involved in the disbursement of subsidies. "Public relations" – with government and bureaucracies, rather than with the general public – becomes the key to success. Crucial factors in market success, such as price and quality competitiveness, speed of delivery, product durability, and so forth, become secondary concerns. Company efforts become increasingly – and in some companies almost, totally – devoted to political lobbying, at the cost of more socially-productive business endeavours. The executive that rises to the top, at least in the subsidy-maximising concerns, is the astute diplomat with bureaucratic/government contacts, not the able and market-orientated businessman.

Secondly, these developments are inevitably accompanied by a swing towards the "administration function", and overhead costs thereof, in industrial management.

Thirdly, firms may choose – on straight grounds of profit-maximization – to operate at a lower level of industrial efficiency than they could achieve, where the inefficiency generates subsidy returns that are larger than the profits that may be derived from efficient conduct.

Fourthly, as Finger's study finds, managers are likely to become less cautious in their evaluation of investment projects that might put the viability of the company (in terms of market revenue and costs) at risk. This will also increase the number of candidates for government subsidization.

Fifthly, as more and more companies cotton on to the possibilities for profit from the subsidy morass, the growing competition for subsidies by political lobbying amongst firms starts to cancel each other's efforts out. The net result will be a zero or insignificant redistribution of profits amongst firms, but a large increase in political lobbying by all firms, and a considerable increase in the size of the government bureaucracy that deals with industry. The only qualification to this proposition is that small firms are generally likely to lose out at the expense of large firms, as there tend to be large economies of scale in lobbying activity.

In Israel these inefficiencies eventually became so intractable that the government had to undertake a two-year crack-down on entire "parasite industries" that had emerged as the long-term result of the subsidy morass (i.e. let them fold).

The supposed rationale of many industrial subsidies is 'to rescue industrial invalids and restore them to health' (Cripps, 1976). The available evidence indicates to the contrary that the long-term effect of extensive subsidization is to weaken the general level of business efficiency, and to increase the number of 'industrial invalids'.

The Long-Term Effects on Employee and Union Behaviour

Employees, and thus their union representatives, are interested not only in wages and working conditions but in the degree of job security that they have. This element of the employment relation may be only partly specified in the form of labour contract documentation. Recent research by labour economists suggests that firms also make unwritten "implicit contracts" with employees concerning their job security. The terms of an implicit contract are signalled to prospective and current employees by the firms' treatment, in the present and the past, of employees who are surplus to requirements (due to economic or technological change, and so forth). As a result, firms build up a reputation for the degree of job security they offer in the mix of net advantages from employment. This may range from virtual tenure (as in Japanese industrial corporations and the British Civil Service) to virtually zero security (as in the harvest labour market in California).

The amount of job security that a firm will implicitly or explicitly offer its employees will depend on a number of factors, such as the volatility of demand for the firms' products, the cost of redundancy to the firm, and *the value which employees put on this job-benefit as against others, such as higher wages.*

As we have seen, a major motive behind the emergence of the subsidy morass is the attempt by governments to preserve jobs, and to prevent or slow the pace of economic adjustments in declining sectors of the economy. The greater the extent and duration of these governmental measures, the smaller will be the relative valuation that employees and unions will put on the job security provided by firms through explicit or implicit agreements. All things being equal, the long-terms effect will be a gradual re-definition of the content of implicit and explicit labour market contracts. Public measures of providing job security through subsidies thus have the long-run effect of reducing the degree of employment security provided by firms. Whether the net amount of job security that obtains after all these adjustments have taken place will have risen, fallen or remain unchanged, is a moot point.

A further consequence is that the lower relative valuation put by employees on the job security provided by firms conversely implies a greater preference for higher wages *vis-à-vis* more stable employment prospects. That is, trades unions will become that much less concerned with the potentially deleterious consequences of their wage demands for the employment prospects of their members, once they have fully understood the implications of the subsidy morass, and the political biasses that have generated it. They are likely to become even more intransigent to wage reductions in recession, and more reckless in making wage demands in boom phases (Burton, 1977b).

These long-term effects via the labour market reinforce the conclusion of the section above: that the subsidy morass will ultimately increase the number of jobs that need to be 'saved' and the number of candidate firms for bailing-out.

This prediction is consistent with the observable differences in union behaviour and attitudes as between Britain and the U.S.A. In America the government has so far avoided any extensive subsidization of industry (with exceptions such as the 1971 Lockheed *débâcle*). U.S. unions have no deeply-entrenched expectation that the government will step in with subsidies to prop up failing companies to 'save jobs', 'restore industrial invalids to health', to arrest 'cumulative spirals', or anything else. They are consequently generally cautious not to force the wage increases they have negotiated with profitable companies onto those which are in a more parlous state, where the employment prospects of their members would be seriously jeopardised by such an increase. Indeed, they may even be prepared to negotiate the roll-back of a signed and legally-enforceable wage contract under such circumstances (Henle, 1973). But in Britain government subsidization of industry has now become large, and union expectations have become increasingly geared to the belief that the government will always step in with subsidies to prevent the failure of any large company, however wretched its performance. The continuing saga of British Leyland is the predictable result.

The Long-Term Effects on the Process of Economic Evolution

The justification of profits, as usually advanced, is that they are (a) a source of funds for future growth and employment, (b) a reward for risk-taking and organizational endeavour, and (c) they act as a "signal" for firms to expand existent capacity/move into industries where profits are high. But there is a further aspect to the profit system which receives little emphasis in modern economic analysis, let alone establishment thinking about the economy, yet which is a central and vital feature of real-world capitalist economies. The system of profit and loss is the mainspring of the ceaseless process of "economic natural selection" or "economic evolution" that operates in a capitalist economy.[29]

The process of natural selection operates in the following fashion: *only those firms which achieve positive profits survive.* Firms that fail to earn profits disappear via compulsory liquidation or voluntary wind-up. In this way the process of economic natural selection in the capitalist economic system mimics the evolutionary processes of nature. Here also "mutations" occur – firms with new products, new concepts of industrial relations, new techniques, new managerial ideas – and are subject to the discipline of natural selection: those mutations which fail to generate positive profits cease to exist. In this way the relatively inefficient, atrociously managed, and financially unsound business organizations gradually fade out over time. This process of economic natural selection in the capitalist economy plays the vital role of weeding out inefficient organizations and maintaining overall economic dynamism (by allowing the profitable business mutations to survive). Putting it differently, it is not only the making of profits, but also the *making of losses,* which performs a vital role in the capitalist economic system. Without losses, economic natural selection could not occur, and inefficient organizations would continue to survive. It is the absence of, a failure to provide a surrogate for, the bankruptcy mechanism of the capitalist economy that ultimately constitutes the most serious economic problem of collectivist economic systems (Nutter, 1968).

The subsidy morass inevitably impairs and distorts the process of economic natural selection. "Saving jobs" in bankrupt firms, providing "assistance" to declining industries, "restoring industrial invalids" to health, and the like, all prevent this process of economic evolution from working. Proponements of industrial subsidies for bankrupt firms, such as Robin Murray (1972) of Sussex university, argue that this is acceptable, on the grounds that the process of economic natural selection is too unselective in its workings: efficient as well as inefficient firms get selected out. Government subsidies should be given to efficient, but temporarily illiquid, firms to get them over short-run difficulties.

Corporate bankruptcy arises when a company has insufficient revenue and money in the till to meet its bills – it has, that is, a "cash-flow problem". Murray's argument is that 'cash flow problems do not necessarily reflect corporate inefficiency'. They may arise because of conditions *external* to the firm – changes in the structure and level of prices, the pattern of demand, the cost and availability of credit or raw materials, etc. – or because of unanticipated *internal* problems (such as an insurmountable design problem), which are in no way related to its technical efficiency in production. Thus economic natural selection weeds out efficient as well as inefficient companies.

The logic of this argument is badly mistaken. An ability to forecast uncertain (external or internal) events correctly or to adjust quickly to them once they occur, is just as much an important survival characteristic for a firm as is its technical efficiency; these factors are an element of genuine overall *economic* efficiency. Murray's argument rests on the fallacious confusion of the concepts of economic and technical efficiency. And it is economic efficiency, not technical efficiency, which is the appropriate yardstick by which to measure a company's performance.

Furthermore, firms that do have a cash flow problem are not necessarily liquidated. If they look sound-enough long-run propositions, they will be able to borrow working capital on the money market to tide them over their short-run illiquidity. Murray's argument on this point is the hoary old chestnut (already dealt with in Chapter II) that the money market is "imperfect":

> the size of the cash deficit may be such that banks and the stock market may adopt a conservative attitude towards risk in the project . . .
> There are a range of cash flows, liquidity, and gearing ratios which the banks and money market does not like to see exceeded without good reason (Murray, 1972).

Yes indeed: not without *good reason*. Lenders adopt these decision rules because hard experience teaches that there is serious prospect of loan repayment default (and thus of their own bankruptcy) where such ranges have been exceeded.[30]

The distortion of the process of economic evolution by the subsidy morass must be seen for what it is: an undeniable sapping of the well-springs of economic progress.

The Long-Term Effects on Government-Industry Relations

The continued existence of a subsidy morass in industry will, in the long rung, generate forces that are likely to bring about even greater government intervention in industry. This follows in part from our analysis above. First, the demand for subsidies will rise as more firms come to compete with others in political lobbying for subsidy disbursements. Trade unions, and groups of workers (via factory "sit-ins"), are also likely to play the same game: indeed this is already happening. Secondly, the deleterious side-effects of subsidization on business efficiency and union wage policy will increase the number of 'industrial invalids' that are candidates for subsidization, and with each there will arise the same political pressures that have led governments into disastrous rescue operations in the past. Thus both the demand and supply of industrial subsidies are likely to increase as the politico-economic system adjusts to the present subsidy morass.

It is also likely to bring about increasing government intervention in forms other than subsidies. First, the deleterious consequences of continued subsidization on business efficiency and union behaviour, and the gradual sapping of the process of economic evolution, will force governments to try to stimulate greater efficiency in subsidized concerns by means of exhortation. And as exhortation has a poor track record as an instrument of government economic policy, we may expect that eventually threats of subsidy withdrawal will have to be made by government in order to instil some greater orientation towards efficiency in subsidized companies. In other words, the long-term effect will be to bring government into direct confrontation with industry and unions in subsidized companies over the issues of efficiency, work productivity, and wage demands. Furthermore, for threats to be believed, they have to be carried out. It is no good rattling the stick in the cupboard if the pupils believe that the teacher is never going to actually bring it out and use it. So, eventually, it will be necessary for governments to force some of the *very adjustments* on industries that subsidies were supposed to avoid. If the validity of this prognosis be doubted, consider the saga of British Leyland. In 1975 the Ryder Report recommended a £1.4b. injection of taxpayers' money over the next 5–6 years into this ailing large firm, an immediate £100m. of which was necessary to pay off the exceptional loans that had kept the company afloat in that year. The basic objective was the "saving" of 170,000 jobs in the company (at what cost of jobs displaced and crowded-out elsewhere is unknown). In 1976 the company lost one-sixth of its planned production, through some 700 disputes and low productivity, and in 1977 started with disastrous levels of output and productivity. As this saga has unfolded, government and NEB commentary has turned from exhortation to criticism to threat of withholding public money. Threat has succeeded threat, with no apparent readiness on the part of the government to actually carry them out. And all the while the company has come nearer and nearer to technical insolvency. So much, then, for the jolly idea of 'temporary subsidies at very high rates in order to rescue industrial invalids and restore them to health' (Cripps, 1976). Now, in 1978, the government has finally been forced to agree to a corporate restructuring involving a run-down of 12,500 jobs in the company (which may be only the start of the process). The British Leyland saga is a portent of things to come: we may expect more 'confrontation scenarios' between government and subsidised industry.

A second way in which the subsidy morass is likely to generate other forms of government intervention lies in the great possibilities which it provides for government to promote its other policy goals. There is a strong temptation for a government to wield the stick of threatened subsidy withdrawal to make companies adopt certain policies which the government has not in fact enacted in statutory legislation. The Labour government's non-statutory incomes policy of 1978 was enforced by such backdoor methods, involving a "blacklist" of companies that have not complied with the government's non-statutory decrees. In other words, the subsidy system provides tempting opportunities for discretionary government intervention on corporatist lines.

Finally, the more that private industry ends up "on the dole" of taxpayers' money, and is perceived to be so by the voter, the more strident and the more legitimate will become the demand of left-wing political figures such as Mr Benn for "public" (i.e., state) participation (i.e., partial or full control) of the firms or industries receiving subsidies. Given the inevitable swings of the electoral pendulum, if the subsidy morass persists we may eventually expect to see these demands acceded to, involving planning agreements, government equity stakes, or full nationalization of subsidized concerns and industries.[31] The subsidy morass, then, reinforces existing tendencies towards the emergence of a collectivist/corporatist state (Pahl and Winkler, 1974).

The Long-Term Effects on the International Economy and Polity
The past thirty years have seen increasing economic interdependence amongst national (developed *and* less-developed) economies, as the result of rapid improvements in transport and communications, successive rounds of tariff reductions under the General Agreement on Tariffs and Trade (GATT), and other factors. Given this pervasive interdependence it is not only tariffs, quotas, and export subsidies that can have international repercussions. Subsidies provided for ostensibly domestic reasons, such as jobs, industrial regeneration, or regional "imbalance" can have pervasive international effects. For example, in 1973,
the Canadian government and the provincial government of Novia Scotia provided incentives to the Michelin Tyre Company – including cash grants, low interest loans, and reductions in local property tax liabilities – so that the firm could establish production facilities in an economically depressed region. But 80 per cent of the plant's production was destined for export (Walker, 1976).
Such examples can be multiplied endlessly. The general point is that, in a highly-interdependent world economy, all domestic subsidies are likely to have effects on industrial and employment prospects in other countries, through distortion of export patterns, the location decisions of internationally-mobile firms, and import-competition.
The problem is not simply that domestic subsidies can distort the pattern of international trade and investment, and reduce the gains from an efficient international division of labour. The attempt to deal with domestic problems via subsidies, without regard to their international repercussions, clearly invites countervailing measures – parallel subsidies, or tariffs – by other countries, so that the world descends into a mutually frustrating system of beggar-my-neighbour domestic policies.

56

This prospect is not fanciful. 'There appears to be general consensus amongst observers . . . that, almost worldwide, public subsidies to industry are growing, in terms of scope and impact' (Malmgren, 1977). In some world-wide industries such as shipbuilding and steel, this international subsidy competition to sustain domestic industry at the expense of other countries has reached intense, not to say bizarre, levels, and now sustains a chronic situation of world over-capacity and production of these commodities. Moreover, competition via subsidies to attract the new plant investments of major international companies has become naked to the point of virtual indecency in some instances:

> When Ford recently announced that it would be building an engine plant in South Wales, officials openly admitted that Britain had outbid other European countries in the (subsidy) terms it had been able to offer. Of the £180m. investment at least £36m. will come from regional government grants.[32]

The United States has so far managed to avoid being dragged very far into this intensifying subsidy competition, but is increasingly (and strongly) resorting to other countervailing measures, such as retaliatory duties, voluntary quotas (shoes and colour TV sets) and reference-price duty systems (steel), to offset the subsidy measures of other countries (Krauss, 1978). This intensifying subsidy competition and retaliation now clearly poses a grave threat to the stability of the international economic and political order. Two quotations from eminent sources may convey the seriousness with which this prospect is now viewed:

> the spread of protectionist measures . . . has reached a point at which the continued existence of an international order, based on agreed and observed rules, may be said to be open to question.[33]
>
> The world is now, nearer sliding back into the protectionism of the 1930s than at any other time for the last 30 years . . . the protectionism which stifled trade and kept millions on the dole 40 years ago is now being presented in a new guise, with seductive modern rational-sounding slogans . . . [34]

. . . like "job preservation", "restoring industrial invalids to health", "the promotion of structural change", and "industrial regeneration". The protectionism of the 1930s exhibited itself mainly in the open and direct form of tariff barriers. The emerging "new protectionism" of the 1970s primarily takes the "backdoor" form of the subsidy morass and other non-tariff barriers to trade. For this very reason it is even more dangerous than the 1930s-style protectionism as a threat to order in a world economy.

Conclusion

The long-term consequences for the economy and polity of a continuing regime of extensive and growing subsidies to industry are bleak. Far from offering the prospect of industrial regeneration, the continuation of this regime is likely to bring about long-term changes in the workings of the economic system that are highly counter-productive. These long-term economic effects are in turn likely to draw forth even greater government intervention in industry, and thus to add a further push in the direction of some collectivist or corporatist order. The long-term international repercussions are equally frightening. Here the prospect is that growing subsidization of industry, undertaken for domestic political reasons, will lead to an intensifying international situation of countervailing non-tariff and tariff measures, leading to general economic stagnation and rupture of international relations. It bears repetition that this prospect is no flight of fancy: it is emerging here and now.

V. On Escaping the Morass

As the preceding Chapter makes clear, a continuation along the present path of extensive government subsidization is folly. It will generate economic and political forces that drag the economic system even further into the morass.

A clear and unavoidable policy choice now has to be made. Either we continue on the present path the "new" industrial strategy, job preservation, etc., – or we switch over to a "social market economy" system as practised in West Germany. Under this latter arrangement, government intervention in the economic process is not entirely excluded, but is acceptable only if such actions are conformable with competitive market arrangements. Policies designed to reduce or remove monopoly and cartels, to reduce barriers to entrepreneurship and entry to industry, are deemed "conformable". Industrial subsidies are, generally, taken to be "non-conformable".

But how can we switch over from the present "mixed-up economy", as the late Professor Harry G. Johnson so scathingly described it, to a social market economy – given the size of the subsidy morass, the vested interests in its maintenance, the political biases that sustain it, and the temporary dislocations that would occur as a result of its sudden elimination?

Some Positive Policy Proposals

First, the proclivity of government to indulge in economically myopic policies in order to buy votes with public money must be curtailed. In other words, the ability of government to reap short-term political profit or itself by exploitation of fiscal illusion must be checked. The voter must be made more aware of the true cost of public spending, so that there is less political incentive for governments to indulge in socially wasteful subsidy expenditures. As the most serious degree of fiscal illusion concerns that component of public expenditure which is deficit-financed, this is where the problem needs to be most urgently tackled. The solution is that constitutional limitations must be placed on the ability of governments to run persistent budget deficits (Buchanan and Wagner, 1977; Buchanan, Burton and Wagner, 1978).

Secondly, a primary and urgent task must be the negotiation of international agreements – both at the level of the EEC, OECD and GATT – to contain and dismantle the growth of the subsidy morass (and other non-tariff trade distortions). This is a pressing matter in and of itself, in view of the threat to international economic and political order posed by the spreading back-door protectionism of domestic industrial subsidies. Furthermore, it will be that much easier in domestic political terms to dismantle the subsidy morass if this is conducted within an internationally-agreed framework. A multilateral agreement to reduce non-tariff or tariff distortion is much easier for domestic politicians to sell to their electors than a unilateral one. There is also the successful prior example of the successive rounds of tariff-cutting conducted under the GATT from 1947 onwards to point to.

The precise content of an international agreement constraining subsidy and related trade distortions, and the best negotiating strategy to attain it, are complex and lengthy topics that cannot be treated here in detail.[35] An essential requirement of the code, however, must be that it draws a clear distinction between a "permitted" category of subsidy measures that have zero or minimal effects on international trade and investment, and a "prohibited" category of those which do not. Furthermore, there must be a realistic system of penalties against transgressions, and a working arbitration procedure.

The forms of subsidization which should be internationally prohibited, in particular, are those which are designed to prevent or slow down economic adjustments, or to "modernize" industry faced with overseas competition. In principle, permissible forms of adjustment assistance would be schemes designed to promote speedier adaptation to market realities and the transference of resources out of declining sectors and firms. This is conformable in theory with the concept of a social market economy. However, even this form of governmental subsidization needs careful international monitoring. For, as Geöran Ohlin has noted, whatever the supposed nature of such measures, '. . . adjustment assistance seems *in practice* often designed to bolster the defences against imports rather than to clear the ground for them'. (Ohlin, 1975; italics added).

A third set of policy measures that will considerably ease the transference from the mixed-up economy of the subsidy morass to a social market economy are those designed to restore the profit motive. With an expansion of profits will come a re-expansion of employment opportunities. And the more that jobs are 'naturally created' through the normal channels of fulfilling consumer demand, the weaker will be the vested producer interest demand for job-preservation and shoring-up measures. Furthermore, the available evidence suggests that a restoration of profits from their present low levels (in real terms) is a much cheaper method of reducing unemployment – both nationally and regionally – than subsidies (Morley, 1976).

This does not mean that the economy should be artificially restimulated by reflationary deficit finance. Profits, followed by employment, would rise temporarily – but only at the expense of higher unemployment later on. Actions are needed to restore the profit incentive in a more sensible and permanent way – the removal of prices, incomes and dividend controls, cuts in the higher marginal rate of personal taxation, the dismantling of the entangling web of pettifogging regulations that now enmeshes British business, and so forth.

Fourthly, if any form of adjustment assistance is to be internationally permitted, it should give assistance to displayed employees, and not to declining firms and/or industries. If we are to allow "the profit system" to operate then the *quid pro quo* must be that "the loss system" of economic natural selection must also be allowed to operate. The social role of profits is a reward for the taking of risks with personal savings and career prospects: but owners must expect to bear the risks if we allow them to collect the returns.

Even so, the form and level of any adjustment assistance to displaced employees must be carefully considered. As the policy goal is the speeding of transference of displaced employees with "old" skills to other sectors of the economy where "new" skills are likely to be required, the emphasis should be on adaptation of skills rather than redundancy payments. That is, the emphasis should lie with the provision of retraining facilities, or retraining "vouchers" which could be used to obtain retraining at either a government training centre or a private or public commercial enterprise. Redundancy compensation is less likely to overcome the problems of skill adaptation caused by structural change, although it may, of course, be effective as a device for overcoming the political problem of vested producer group resistance to economic change. A further problem with state-financed redundancy payments as a form of adjustment assistance, however, is that they may actually inhibit economic adjustment. That is, the higher the level of redundancy payments, the less ready employees in ailing firms will be to accept internal adjustments that promote greater efficiency and viability. The Shipbuilding Redundancy Payments Bill of 1978 is a case in point. This provides for *tax-free* compensation to redundant shipyard workers of up to £10,400 per man – a rate of compensation about three times that available under the national redundancy payments scheme. It is perhaps not surprising that suicidal industrial disputes such as that at the Swan Hunter yard – which caused the loss of prospective Polish ship orders and the announcement of 1,152 redundancies – happen in such a context.

Fifthly, there is a case for re-examining the workings of the legal process of corporate liquidation, to see if this cannot be improved. There is a large degree of public misunderstanding about corporate bankruptcy. Take, for example, the following statement attributed to a Conservative ex-Minister:

> Market forces would mean the end of British Leyland, Chrysler and British Steel. It's not like chicken-farming . . . find some eggs, sit on them and start all over again. Once they're gone, they're gone, what's destroyed can never be rebuilt . . .[36]

This sort of statement – which is not unrepresentative of widely-held beliefs – displays a considerable degree of misunderstanding of the economics of bankruptcy. First, when a firm goes into liquidation the physical assets of the company are not 'destroyed' – they are simply *revalued* downwards. If British Leyland or British Steel (etc.) were liquidated their car assembly plants and steel rolling mills would remain. The purpose of the downward revaluation is to find a purchaser for the assets of the company. And the assets are usually more valuable if they are sold together – as a complete working organization, or perhaps as a number of separate working plants – than separately, as a large number of separate lots of equipment, buildings, etc. Thus, for instance, if British Leyland were to be liquidated, the likelihood is that a large part of the present company would remain in operation, in the hands of new owners (perhaps, however, split up into a number of smaller companies).

However, the more speedily the winding-up proceeds, the easier it is to sell as a complete working organization, with a full complement of trained managerial personnel and skilled employees. It is not impossible to visualise ways in which the workings of the bankruptcy mechanism could be improved, so that the likelihood of organizational maintenance of bankrupt enterprises is enhanced. One possibility along these lines that deserves serious consideration is Sam Brittan's suggestion of

an agency to take an active part in breaking-up insolvent concerns into smaller components, with perhaps some public funds to prevent a chain reaction among suppliers and creditors, and to avoid sudden mass dismissals of labour while new owners are being sought (Brittan, 1975b)

Finally, government should avoid adding to the problems of economic adjustment by the promotion of mergers with taxpayer's money. What these ill-conceived measures have usually boiled down to in reality, as Professor Caves noted in the Brookings Institution study of the British economy, is a strategy of 'finding the most efficient firm and merging the rest into it' (Caves, 1968). The more efficient firms are then lumbered with the burden of the less-efficient and dragged down with them. Furthermore, the problem of eventual adjustment to market realities is made that much more difficult – the omelette that has eventually to be unscrambled is that much larger. The formation of British Leyland from a number of previously independent car manufacturers, for instance, was originally the result of the IRC's attempt to "restructure, rationalize and regenerate" the British car industry. Now the task of unscrambling this governmental creation will have to begin. Things would have been easier if it had never interfered in the first place! The general point is that the political, economic and social problems arising from economic adjustment in the form of the contraction or disappearance of ailing enterprises are the more difficult the larger the size of the organization concerned. Government should not actively add to these problems by the artificial promotion of mergers.

Conclusion

Things have not yet gone so far that an escape from the subsidy morass and its consequences is impossible. But things have certainly gone so far in Britain and, indeed, more generally in the world economy, that a choice cannot be evaded much longer – either domestically or internationally. The attempt to solve problems of employment, efficiency and growth with a morass of government subsidies will eventually bring about – indeed, is now bringing about – long-run economic and political responses that will deepen the very problems with which the measures were supposed to deal.

FOOTNOTES

1. Full references for all sources cited are given in the bibliography at the end of this monograph.

2. Some of the items listed are now, of course, inoperative.

3. *Public Expenditure to 1979–80*, Cmnd. 6393, London: HMSO. Projections for expenditures in future years contained in this document are omitted.

4. The 1977 and 1978 PESC White Papers (*The Government's Expenditure Plans*, Vol. II, Cmnd. 6721-II, February, 1977; and *The Government's Expenditure Plans, 1978–79 to 1981–82*, Cmnd. 7049-II, January, 1978) might superficially appear to reveal a slackening in the growth of the subsidy morass. A closer inspection shows that subsidies and loans to private industry, and Manpower Services Commission expenditures, have continued to grow apace, but have been roughly offset by the elimination of the massive subsidies to nationalized industries (compensation for price controls) initiated by the Heath administration during 1972–74.

5. *The Regeneration of British Industry*, Cmnd. 5710, London: HMSO, 1974.

6. *An Approach to Industrial Strategy*, Cmnd. 6315, London: 1975.

7. Labour Party Conference Address, 28 September 1976.

8. For a thoughtful appraisal of the post-war orthodoxy in employment policy, see Brittan (1975a).

9. See, for example, M. Corina, "A Subsidy Which Has Kept 200,000 at Work", *The Times*, 31 March 1977, p.21.

10. This issue is explained in greater detail in Chapter IV.

11. The issues in the 'crowding-out' debate involve complex issues of economic model specification, and little purpose would be served by pursuing these in detail here. The interested reader or student is referred to Carlson and Spencer (1975) for a brief survey, and the literature therein cited.

12. According to the latest figures (December 1977), the TES scheme covers some 364,366 employees at 5,621 companies, at an annual cost of approximately £400m. a year. The six-month supplement covers 42,700 employees at 550 plants.

13. Another point to be noted is that some subsidies have worked out at somewhat greater than 30 per cent of the average industrial wage. Jones' (1977) calculations suggest that the subsidies given to set up a primary aluminium smelting industry in the UK worked out at a cool £200,000 per job!

14. Studies in the USA suggest that between 40 and 60 per cent of all job changers lose no working time in switching from one employment to another.

15. *Labour Party General Election Manifesto,* London: The Labour Party, 1964.

16. The origins of such a policy lie even further back in time, in the form of the National Research Development Corporation (NRDC) established by the Attlee administration in 1948. It was the Wilson Administration of 1964–69, however, that was first to put major emphasis on this type of sectoral policy.

17. *Industrial Expansion,* Cmnd. 3509, London: HMSO, 1968

18. For an in-depth analysis of this particular sectoral policy, see Jones (1977).

19. Entrepreneurs will doubtless be stimulated to prodigious acts of expansion by the fact that the DoI sends a large, multi-coloured wall-map of the "assisted" areas to all applicants for this "free" booklet.

20. *An Approach to Industrial Strategy,* Cmnd. 6315, London: HMSO, 1975.

21. See Burton (1978).

22. *Industrial Expansion,* Cmnd. 3509, London: HMSO, 1968.

23. *The prospects for the United Kingdom Computer Industry in the 1970s,* House of Commons Paper 621, Session 1970–71, London: HMSO, 1971.

24. A brief review of this fast-developing area of the economics of politics is provided by Tullock (1976).

25. Puviani (1897).

26. For more detailed discussion see Buchanan and Wagner (1976); Buchanan, Burton and Wagner (1978).

27. This important factor was explored first by Downs (1957).

28. Consultants specializing in advice, and acquisition of, government subsidies are now beginning to appear in the UK, See, for example, 'Advice on Getting Grants', *Observer,* February 5th, 1978, p.15.

29. This concept, as with so much else in modern economics, owes its conception to the insightful analysis of Professor Armen Alchian (1951).

30. It is worth noting that the particular purpose of Murray's (1972) argument was to justify the shoring-up of Upper Clyde Shipbuilders with taxpayers' money, on the assumption that there was 'still unproven long-run world over-capacity' in shipbuilding. One wonders what Mr. Murray would say now – with even the efficient Japanese, Swedish and West German yards accepting that large capacity cutbacks are inevitable. A sober antidote to Murray's mixture of mistaken analysis and optimistic prognosis is provided by Broadway (1976).

31. The provision of government subsidies has, of course, been used as a justification for nationalization in many past instances.

32. *Investment in Britain: A Survey,* London: *The Economist,* November, 1977, p.65

33. *International Trade* 1976–77, Geneva: GATT Secretariat.

34. E.E.C. Commission Vice President Wilhelm Haferkemp *European Community*, No. 8, October, 1977, page 16.

35. For detailed discussion, see Corden (1976), Curzon and Curzon (1972), Denton and O'Cleireacain (1972), Fels (1974), Lloyd (1974), Malmgren (1977), O'Cleireacain (1972), Tumlir (1974), and Walker (19 ¡ 6).

36. Quoted in G. Turner, "Is it Counter-Revolution – or Consensus?" *Daily Telegraph*, 12 October 1977, p.16.

REFERENCES

ALCHIAN, A. (1951)   "Uncertainty, Evolution and Economic Theory", *Journal of Political Economy*, Vol. 58, No. 3, June, pp.211-221.

BRITTAN, S. (1975a)   *Second Thoughts on Full Employment Policy*, London: Centre for Policy Studies.

BRITTAN, S. (1975b)   *Participation without Politics: An Analysis of the Nature and Role of Markets*, London: Institute of Economic Affairs.

BROADWAY, F. (1976)   *Upper Clyde Shipbuilders*,London: Centre for Policy Studies.

BUCHANAN J. M. and WAGNER, R. E. (1977)   *Democracy in Deficit: Lord Keynes Legacy to America*, New York: Academic Press.

BUCHANAN, J. M., BURTON, J. and WAGNER, R. E. (1978)   *The Consequences of Mr. Keynes*, London: Institute of Economic Affairs.

BURTON, J. (1977a)   "Employment Subsidies – The Cases For and Against", *National Westminster Bank Quarterly Review*, February, pp.33-43.

BURTON, J. (1977b)   "Depression Unemployment, Union Wage Rigidity, and Employment Subsidies", *International Journal of Social Economics*, Vol. 4, No. 1, pp.48-54.

BURTON. J. (1977c)   "A Micro-economic Analysis of Employment Subsidy Programmes", *Human Resources Workshop Paper 9* (mimeo), Kingston-upon-Thames: Kingston Polytechnic, School of Economics and Politics.

BURTON, J. (1978) — "Social Costs and Public Policy", in CHEUNG, S.C. *et al*, *The End of Social Cost?*, London: Institute of Economic Affairs.

BYATT, I (1976) — "The Economic Rationale of Subsidies to Industry: Comment", in A. WHITING (1976a), *op. cit.*, pp.75–76.

CAIRNCROSS, A. (1970) — "The Managed Economy", in CAIRNCROSS (*ed.*), *The Managed Economy*, Oxford: Basil Blackwell.

CARLSON, K. M. and SPENCER, R. W. (1975) — "Crowding Out and Its Critics", *Federal Reserve Bank of St. Louis Review*, Vol. 57, No. 12, Dec., pp.2–17.

CAVES, R. E. (1968) — "Market Organization, Performance, and Public Policy", in R. E. CAVES and Associates, *Britain's Economic Prospects*, London: Allen and Unwin, pp.279–323.

CORBETT, H. and JACKSON, R. (eds.), (1974) — *In Search of a New World Economic Order*, London: Croom Helm in association with the Trade Policy Research Centre.

CORDEN, W. M. and FELS, G. (1976) — *Public Assistance to Industry: Protection and Subsidies in Britain and Germany*, Macmillan for the Trade Policy Research Centre.

CORDEN, W. M. (1976) — "Conclusions on the logic of Government Intervention", in CORDEN and FELS, *op. cit.*, pp.215–229.

CRIPPS, T. F. (1976) — "The Economics of Labour Subsidies", in A. WHITING (1976a), *op. cit.*, pp.105–108.

CURZON, G. and CURZON, V. (1972) — *Global Assault on Non-Tariff Trade Barriers*, London: Trade Policy Research Centre.

DANIEL, W. W. (1972) — *Whatever Happened to the Workers of Woolwich?: A Survey of Redundancy in South-East London*, London: Political and Economic Planning.

DENTON, G. (1976) — "Financial Assistant to British Industry", in CORDEN and FELLS, *op. cit.*, pp.120–164.

DENTON, G. and O'CLEIREACAIN, S. (1972) — *Subsidy Issues in International Commerce*, London: Trade Policy Research Centre.

DENTON, G.
O'CLEIREACAIN, S. and
ASH, S. (1975)

Trade Effects of Public Subsidies to Private Enterprise, London: Macmillan for the Trade Policy Research Centre.

DEPARTMENT OF
EMPLOYMENT (1977a)

"Surveys Carried Out into Special Employment Schemes", *Department of Employment Gazette*, July, pp.692–696.

DEPARTMENT OF
EMPLOYMENT (1977b)

"Duration of Unemployment and Age of Unemployed", *Department of Employment Gazette*, August.

DEPARTMENT OF
EMPLOYMENT AND
PRODUCTIVITY (1968)

"The Duration of Unemployment", *Department of Employment and Productivity Gazette*, August.

DEPARTMENT OF
INDUSTRY (1976)

Incentives for Industry in the Areas for Expansion, London: HMSO, December.

DOWNS, A. (1957)

An Economic Theory of Democracy, New York: Harper and Row.

EXPENDITURE COMMITTEE
(1971–2)

Public Money in the Private Sector, 6th Report from the Expenditure Committee, House of Commons Paper 347, Session 1971–2, Volume I, Report. Volumes II and III, Minutes of Evidence.

FELS, G. (1974)

"Adjustment Assistance to Import Competition", in CORBET and JACKSON, *op. cit.*, pp.245–259.

FINGER, N (1974)

The Impact of Government Subsidies on Industrial Management: The Israeli Experience, New York: Praeger.

GARDNER, N. K.
(1976)

"The Economics of Launching Aid", in A. WHITING (1976) *op. cit.*, pp. 141–155.

GINZBERG, E. (*et al*)
(1976)

Re-examining European Manpower Policies, Washington, D.C.: National Commission for Manpower Policy.

GREENWOOD, J. (1977)

Worker Sit-Ins and Job Protection, Westmead, Farnborough: Gower Press.

HARTLEY, K. (1975)

"Industry, Labour and Public Policy", in GRANT, R. M. and SHAW, G. K. (eds.), *Current Issues in Economic Policy*, Deddington, Oxford: Philip Allan, pp.34–60

HARTLEY, K (1976)

"The Economics of Labour Subsidies: Comment", in A. WHITING (1976a), *op. cit.*, pp. 109–112.

69

HENLE, P. (1973)   "Reverse Collective Bargaining? A Look at Some Union Concession Situations", *Industrial and Labor Relations Review*, Vol. 26, No. 3, April, pp. 956–968.

HINDLEY, B. (1970)   *Industrial Mergers and Public Policy*, London: Institute of Economic Affairs.

JEWKES, J. (1972)   *Government and High Technology*, London: Institute of Economic Affairs.

JONES, C. (1977)   *The £200,000 Job!*, London: Centre for Policy Studies.

KRAUSS, M. B. (1978)   "Stagnation and the 'New Protectionism' ", *Challenge*, Vol. 20, No. 6, pp. 40–44.

LAYARD, P. R. G. and NICKELL, S. J. (1977)   "The Case for Subsidizing Extra Jobs", *London School of Economics Discussion Paper No. 15*, (mimeo), London: L.S.E., Centre for Labour Economics.

LLOYD, P. (1974)   "Strategies for Modifying Non-Tariff Distortions" in CORBETT and JACKSON, *op. cit.*, pp. 199–210.

MACKAY, D. I. (1972)   "After the Shake-Out", *Oxford Economic Papers*, Vol. 24, No. 1

MALMGREN, H. B. (1977)   *International Order for Public Subsidies*, London: Trade Policy Research Centre.

MORLEY, R. (1976)   "Unemployment, Profits' Share and Regional Policy", in A. WHITING, (176a), *op. cit.*, pp. 159–182.

MUKHERJEE, S. (1976a)   *Unemployment Costs . . .*, London: Political and Economic Planning.

MUKHERJEE, S. (1976b)   *Government and Labour Markets: Aspects of Policies in Britain, France, Germany, Netherlands and Italy*, London: Political and Economic Planning.

MURRAY, R. (1972)   UCS: *The Anatomy of Bankruptcy*, Nottingham: Spokesman Books.

NUTTER, G. W. (1968)   "Markets without Property: The Grand Illusion", in N. BEADLES and L. DREWERY, Jr., (eds.), *Money, The Market and the State*, Athens: University of Georgia Press.

O'CLEIREACAIN, S. (1972)   "Adjustment Assistance to Import Competition", in McFADZEAN, F. (*et al*), *Towards an Open World Economy*, London: Macmillan for the Trade Policy Research Centre, pp.137–154.

OHLIN, G. (1969)   "Trade in a Non-Laissez Faire World", in SAMUELSON, P.A. (*ed.*), *International Economic Relations*, London: Macmillan.

OHLIN, G. (1975)   *Adjustment for Trade, Studies on Industrial Adjustment Problems and Policies*, Paris: OECD.

PAHL, R. E. and WINKLER, J. T. (1974)   "The Coming Corporatism", *New Society*, 10 October 1974, pp. 72–76.

PEACOCK, A. (1977)   "Giving Economic Advice in Difficult Times", *Three Banks Review*, No. 113, March, pp.3–23.

PREST, A. R. (1976)   "The Economic Rationale of Subsidies to Industry", in A. WHITING (1976a), *op.cit.*, pp.65–74.

PUVIANI, A. (1897)   *Teoria della illusione nelle entrate publiche*, Perugia.

REHN, G. (1975)   "The Fight Against Stagflation", Stockholm: Swedish Institute for Social Research, (mimeo).

REHN, G. (1976)   "Recent Trends in Western Economies: Needs and Methods for Further Development of Manpower Policy", in GINZBERG, E., *op. cit.*, pp. 53–72.

SHOUP, C. S. (1972)   in *The Economics of Federal Subsidy Programs*, Washington, D.C.: Joint Economic Committee.

STIGLER, G. J. (1967)   "Imperfections in the Capital Market", *Journal of Political Economy*, LXXV, No. 3, June.

TULLOCK, G. (1976)   *The Vote Motive*, London: The Institute of Economic Affairs.

TUMLIR, J. (1974)   "Emergency Protection against Sharp Increases in Imports", In CORBET and JACKSON, *op. cit.*, pp.260–284.

WALKER, W. N. (1976)   *International Limits to Government Intervention in the Market-Place*, London: Trade Policy Research Centre.

WEDDERBURN, D. (1964)   *White-Collar Redundancy: A Case-Study*, London: Cambridge University Press.

WEDDEERBURN, D. (1965)   *Redundancy and the Railwaymen*, London: Cambridge University Press.

WHITING, A. (*ed.*) (1976a)   *The Economics of Industrial Subsidies*, London: HMSO

WHITING, A. (1976b)   "Overseas Experience in the Use of Industrial Subsidies", in WHITING, A. (1976a), *op. cit.*, pp.45–63.

WOOD, J. (1975)   *How Much Unemployment?*, London, Insitute of Economic Affairs.